THE SINGLE PARENT EXPERIENCE

The Single Parent Experience

By Carole Klein

WALKER AND COMPANY
New York

Copyright © 1973 by Carole Klein

All rights reserved. No part of this book may be reproduced or transmitted in any form or by any means, electronic or mechanical, including photocopying, recording, or by any information storage and retrieval system, without permission in writing from the Publisher.

First published in the United States of America in 1973 by the Walker Publishing Company, Inc.

Published simultaneously in Canada by Fitzhenry & Whiteside, Limited, Toronto.

ISBN: 0-8027-0371-2

Library of Congress Catalog Card Number: 72-80536

Printed in the United States of America.

10 9 8 7 6 5 4 3 2 1

Contents

Introduction	5
Why Separate Parenthood from Marriage?	13
The Importance of Being Honest	23
The Single Parent—Male	43
Who Are the Unmarried Mothers of Today?	61
Homosexual Parents	77
Adoption	91
Natural Motherhood	109
The Single Parent's Family	131
Child Care	141
The Social Realities of Being a Single Parent	163
The Alternative Life-Style	179
The Psychological Effects of Having a Single Parent	195
Creating Tomorrow's Person	213
Appendix: State Sources for Adoption, Pregnancy, and Related Legal Counseling	225
Bibliography	239

To my mother, LEE HONIG
A very special parent

*"There are more things in heaven and earth, Horatio,
Than are dreamt of in your philosophy."*

"Oh brave new world, that has such people in it."

Acknowledgments

As I explored the provocative new life-style of single parenthood, many people helped as guides. First of course are all the single parents themselves. Their willingness to share their experiences, their candor in discussing their feelings, gives the book a vitality it could not have had otherwise. I have of course respected their right and desire for anonymity by changing names and certain circumstances. In this way, while reader involvement is not sacrificed, individual parents' identities are protected.

Other people figured less directly, but no less importantly, in telling the story of single parents. I have interviewed countless people in the psychological and sociological fields who helped interpret this story in relation to their own professional experience. My thanks go to each one of them. In particular, I would like to thank Dr. Benjamin Spock. His gracious consent to make room for my questions in a busy schedule is deeply appreciated. Even more appreciated, however, was his total involvement in my project during the course of our meeting. A genuine interest in other people's concerns is rare in any person. In a man of Dr. Spock's stature it is especially remarkable. I am grateful, therefore, not only for the intellectual dimensions he added to my subject, but also because our meeting made me feel richer as a person.

I wish also to thank Dr. Ian Alger, psychiatrist and clinical assistant professor of psychiatry at New York Medical College, New York City. Dr. Alger thought of the title *Marriage, The Great Substitute,* long before I related it to the subject of this book. His ideas on marriage and human relations were invaluable to me.

If one person's thinking could be singled out as having made continuous sense as I sifted through my research, it is that of Dr. Irving Markowitz, psychiatrist and director of the Child Guidance and Family Service Clinic of the Oranges and Maplewood, New Jersey. He is a man of enormous intellectual range, and never fails to bring fresh perspective to an issue. He clings to no doctrine, and is always ready to entertain new ideas. His opinions were particularly relevant to a book that tells the story of people experimenting with innovative lifestyles.

I wish also to thank Dr. Henry Biller, Ph.D., associate professor of psychology, University of Rhode Island. Although we never met, he sent me several research papers dealing with his work on the psychological effects of having only one parent. It was work that greatly contributed to my own investigations on this subject.

Among my first interviewees for the book was Mrs. Francis Agreen of the Family and Children's Service of Monmouth County, New Jersey. Her knowledge served as a base for me to begin my other research. I appreciate her time, and the quality of that time.

All through the research work for this book, I called on the services of Ms. Gwendolyn Davis, librarian for the Child Welfare League in New York City. She invariably had the answer for any question, and many times generated new ideas for me

ACKNOWLEDGMENTS

by the material I was directed to.

Mr. Charles Bates of the Boston Children's Service offered his cooperation, as did T. Richard Flaharty of the Maud Booth Family Center in Los Angeles, California.

To Bernice Goodman, who introduced me to many people important to my research, and who herself contributed valuable insights, I also give sincere words of thanks.

I am indebted to a particular book, *Family in Transition,* edited by Arlene S. Skolnick and Jerome H. Skolnick. They have compiled a comprehensive series of writings on the changing nature of the family. I recommend the book to anyone doing research in this area.

An important word of thanks to Barbara Neilson and Ghislaine Boulanger, my editor, who first saw the story behind the idea of being a single parent. My relationship with Ms. Boulanger is based on mutual respect and continues to be extremely gratifying.

Lastly, affectionate thanks to my family and friends, who put up with my sometimes chaotic schedule. Their interest and support helped make the book possible. More important, however, it made the writing of the book more pleasurable, through my being able to share its development with them.

Carole Klein
New York
July, 1972

Introduction

ONE OF THE POPULAR criticisms of this time we live in is that our experiences have gone beyond our language. Filed in the mind's attic with dusty relics of simpler days are automatic responses to such words as *hero, patriot, moral,* or *success.*

Our grandparents knew what a hero was. Someone who willingly marched off to war to defend his country at the unquestioned risk of his own life. Our fathers knew what success was: accumulated savings, a steady job, and no debts outstanding.

Who is sure enough to offer such definitions today? Is a *hero* someone who fights in Vietnam, or who risks going to prison by refusing to fight? Is a woman *moral* who sticks to a loveless marriage "for the sake of the children?" Or is she moral if she refuses to marry the father of her child because she doesn't truly love him?

This is an age of transition. An age when the cultural definitions of who we are and what we should be are being questioned. The labels that defined us are being peeled off, sometimes cautiously, sometimes with abandon, but there seems little doubt that the language of the labels leaves much unsaid.

Single parent is a label that historically has brought two pictures to mind. In one, the promiscuous, lazy, "fallen woman," and in the other, the noble, gently weeping widow, or even the poor divorcée whose husband callously left her (probably for one of those girls in the first picture!). A great deal has already been written to guide the woman, and also the man, who becomes a single parent through the accident of death or divorce. Society as a rule is very sympathetic and supportive of their fears. We have marvelously soothing answers to help the suddenly single parent adjust to her new responsibility. We assure her or him that they will be able to bring up their child alone, and are often quite willing to tell them how. And so this book will not be addressed to that category of single parent for there are enough voices already speaking in their direction. Nor does the book deal with the stereotype "unwed mother," except hopefully to eliminate the stereotype.

The single parent within these pages is the person who has *chosen* this role. The reasons for the choice are often different. To try to draw some composite picture of the single parent would be to repeat the stereotyping I've already deplored. The book will deal as much with the differences between people who choose single parenthood as with their similarities. Some single parents adopt. Some are men. Some are women. Some are young, some are quite a bit older. Some are black, some are white. Some girls deliberately become pregnant, often without ever letting a man know he's the father. Others accidentally conceive and decide to go through with the pregnancy even though marriage with the baby's father is not likely.

While those people who become single parents through death or divorce will share some of the problems faced by those who choose the role, the problems of the single-by-choice parent are in many ways unique. The primary reason for this uniqueness has already been alluded to: society's attitude toward their decision. Whether they adopt or have a natural child, they are inviting their culture's more than casual attention. For the single parent, almost by definition, is separating ideas we've always felt were inseparable. Tradition, that comfortable security blanket we are taught to hide behind, says marriage and parenthood go together—baby makes three, not two. Mothers are first wives, and fathers are first husbands, and families consist of a man and a woman and children. NOT a man OR a woman and a child.

So the man who brings his adopted child home to his casually furnished apartment, and the mother who sets up a crib in her husbandless bedroom may find that, unlike the brave widow or widower, their own brand of courage goes unappreciated.

The picture, of course, is not completely bleak. If it were, there would be no reason for a book about single parents. The story of the single parent is the story of a growing, if grudging, acceptance of variations on our most treasured theme. Like every other aspect of our culture, the family as we knew it is in transition. We are rethinking assumptions on which generations of people have lived, and finding that they were after all only assumptions. For some people, this is terribly exciting. It opens up a tremendous range of possibilities for behavior.

For others, though, it is very confusing, often painfully so, which explains their reluctance to accept such "pioneer" people as the single parent. Many sociologists feel that much interpersonal hostility—between the generations, between the "hardhats" and "long-hairs," or in the bumper-sticker battles of "Another Family for Peace" and "America, Love It or Leave It"—results from the fact that our traditional verities are being questioned. And in the insistent questioning of values long taken for granted, many people are uncomfortably confronting the idea that perhaps the "right" way of life, *their* way of life, was not the right way after all.

The pregnant girl who says she does not need marriage can awaken all kinds of nagging regrets buried deep in the consciousness of a woman dully married for twenty-five years. The idea that her moral code, so grimly endured, is not only not shared but irrelevant to this "cool" new person can loosen the basic foundations of her life. In the name of self-righteous disapproval, she may mask a whole range of emotions, from guilt to envy to fear. Questions nag around the edges of her walled-off virtue. Was it really necessary to have stayed married, to have repressed her instincts? Is this girl going to "get away with" everything she never allowed herself to even dream of? These are soul-searing questions, and the answers are often profoundly disturbing. They burn holes in the blanket of tradition, make belief in agreed upon moral codes less comforting. For if we knew we were not really very happy, at least we knew we were playing by the rules, and there was some pride in that, we were told. But now here are people throwing out the rules, abandoning agreements, playing the game of parenthood on an entirely new board. They are "advancing straight to Go," and going it alone. And what's more, many are being remarkably successful, picking up the new rules as comfortably as if they had always known them. Or even more disturbing to the traditionalists, making up the rules as they go along!

It is really very interesting to see how easily parenthood fits many single parents. It is particularly interesting in contrast with the still somewhat prevalent caricature of the "unwed mother." Not only does this phrase bring flushed cheeks to local legislators, who are convinced she will clutter up the welfare rolls until the day she dies ("breeding like a rabbit all the while"), there is also the assumption that at best, she will treat her motherhood with a cavalier hand. Somehow we have made the connection between unwed natural motherhood and lack of concern for the child involved. We puritanically reject the idea that the human result of a libidinous romp, unblessed by law or clergy, could be anything but an unwelcome "accident."

The term "accident" is, in fact, a very popular euphemism for the baby born to the single parent. And to play a semantic game for a moment, "accident" is not a particularly positive term in our vocabulary. It means we somehow lost control of destiny, often through carelessness or bad judgment, and that we got hurt. So the out-of-wedlock baby becomes the equivalent of the plastered leg of the ski trip, the blistered skin of the tropic beach, the cracked rib of the automobile collision. At best we feel pity for the child, at the worst, contempt.

Continuing the semantic game-playing, a married woman who has a baby is immediately a "parent." An unmarried girl becomes only an unmarried "mother." It is as if responsible parenthood is possible only when two names are signed to a marriage certificate. This is, of course, ridiculous. A marriage certificate does many things. It legalizes adult relationships. It fits into the structures of our society. It provides legal and economic benefits for future children. But it does not automatically turn two people into potentially good parents. Certainly marriage legitimatizes the parental role, but it clearly has nothing to do with how individuals will adjust to that role. A cold, selfish girl does not become a warm, mothering woman because she has signed her name to a piece of paper recognized by the state in which she lives. A man who rejects intimacy, who is uncomfortable with too much responsibility, does not receive these feelings along with his receipt for a marriage license.

And so with this kind of awareness to support their instincts, more and more people are stepping out of the box labeled *marriage and family,* and opting for only *family.* The number of so-called illegitimate children born in this country has risen steadily every year since World War II. In California alone, 46,000 single women gave birth last year. Before we pull out yet another stereotype (poor, black, uneducated), note that the illegitimacy rate for middle-class white people is rising, while the rate for black people continues to decline. What is legitimately significant in these statistics, however, is that well over half of the single, pregnant women who contact social service agencies decide to keep their babies rather than give them up for adoption.

If this cannot yet be called a trend, it certainly indicates a shift in some of our most entrenched social attitudes. Despite some people's angry confusion at how this shift occurred, a glance at our recent history makes it not only understandable, but almost inevitable. The various influences that have fashioned new images of ourselves will be discussed later in the book. I will touch on them briefly here, only to set the stage for the story these images will tell.

A major change in our attitudes and behavior has been a result of the birth control pill, which divorced sex from its traditional link with procreation. Without the specter of unwanted pregnancy hovering over the bed, "morality" took on a different meaning. Men and women at younger and younger ages were free to enjoy each other sexually outside marriage. What's more, they could enjoy sex with people they would not necessarily *want* to marry. Add to the technology of contraception the women's liberation movement, which says women are people first and women second, and that femininity has nothing to do with financial or intellectual dependence on a man. Mix in with these changes the snowballing technology that, even before women's liberation, challenged sex-role definitions of who we are and what it is possible for us, man or woman, to become. For instance, a man can no longer experience his masculinity through the work he does, any more than a woman fulfills her expected role as mother by pounding a washboard. Washing machines and vacuum cleaners have eliminated that way of definition.

And then there is the war, dragging on for years, that has eroded people's faith in the "credibility" of any traditional value system, as well as in the sense that there are any leaders who can really be counted on to protect our personal destinies.

The days when we could sit at the feet of people wiser than ourselves and learn from their experiences are gone. Yesterday's truth is obsolete by the time morning comes, and even people we do respect can, in the light of today's frantic life changes, be no more secure about tomorrow than we are ourselves.

Again, this is both terrifying or liberating depending on what door to tomorrow you walk through. It puts great emphasis on personal truth, on existential experience, on independent values. The "right" way has been replaced by a variety of ways, each of which competes for our attention.

The people in this book have ignored the accepted "fact" that life comes in stages and you must move through one before entering the other. But this does not seem to mean that they take parenthood any less seriously because they have skipped over marriage. Neither are they people who have become so sophisticated about family relationships that they drain them of any emotional intensity, preferring cool reason to any hint of sentiment. On the contrary, whether they are dealing with their children or other adults, many single parents seem particularly committed to making a depersonalized world more human.

Another assumption we may make about single parents is that they are "obviously" narrowing the circle of the nuclear family more than ever before. But in fact, many single parents are pulling in tighter just to get more leverage for jumping out again. And this time, the jump is toward a much wider circle, extending perimeters far beyond where they have stood in the past. When single parents speak of "family," they often have a very different definition in mind. "Family is fluid—as many people who I care about, I consider my family," says one single mother. "People, children or adults, who I share goals with, and whose welfare concerns me, that's a family," says another.

The majority of single parents I interviewed were people concerned with extending family relationships to fit this kind of criteria. Yes, they lived in a family model much of society would consider incomplete, but in reality, many were filling in the model with more people than any nuclear family provides. So many said, in so many different ways, that they wanted their children exposed not to the narrow experiencing of one woman, one man that was the world of their own childhoods, but to a much bigger world filled with several warm, loving people who they could learn to love and trust.

Many single parents have replicated some kind of extended family unit, delighting in its opportunity for diversity. Others speak of moving to a commune or starting one of their own. Even the people who are inclined to live alone with their child generally engage in some kind of cooperative child-care arrangement that makes the single-parent life-style more possible. I will explore all these experiences later in the book.

It will become clear that some people are more successful at this life-style than others. Some are simply more "together" people as well as more capable single parents. Some motives for becoming a single parent are "healthier" than others. It is my aim in this book to illustrate the entire picture, exaggerating neither its deficiencies nor successes. For people who contemplate becoming, or are already single parents, I hope it will be a positive guide. For those readers who are interested in gaining understanding of other people's experiences, I hope the book will provide a reasoned, objective examination from which they can draw their own conclusions.

Why Separate Parenthood from Marriage?

IN THIS TIME of women's liberation, "third world" movements, "swinging marriage," open homosexuality, middle-class dropouts, and student rebellions, yesterday's answers to life's important questions fade quickly away. They seem part of some primitive language that can speak of much simpler issues than we 1973 people are involved with.

Margaret Mead has said that in a changing world we are all immigrants. Like immigrants, many people stand on the edge of the new world and wonder uncertainly where to go next. In periods of rapid change, there are no maps to chart the way. We cannot proceed automatically, one step in front of the other, down familiar paths to predictable destinations.

Like immigrants, we hear voices saying things we have never heard before. The language is new and, again, gives few answers. All we seem to hear are questions. Questions that pierce the validity of our deepest ideas and traditions. And like the immigrant who leaves his customs and old-world methods behind, many men and women trying to respond to this transitional time are turning their backs on the past and beginning a new beginning.

For in many ways it is a beginning. At no time in history have society's precepts and moralities been under as much attack as they are today. Yesterday's "truth" is today's quaint bit of mythology. Tradition is meaningless in a world where the only constant is that nothing stays constant, where the only thing you can count on is change.

When discussing social change, it is very difficult to pinpoint which came first. Did a need create an awareness and demand for change, or did change accelerate consciousness of the need? Is our behavior creating new values, or are we only making our values catch up with new external conditions?

It is, of course, a combination of both. Various external forces have created totally new patterns of living. World War II, for example, disrupted traditional family structures, and the country's easy security became suddenly threatened. The atomic bomb placed a new consciousness on children born under its shadow. Life would never be really certain again, and long-terms goals often seem absurd when measured against imminent destruction.

Other technology caused its own explosions, making some of our most basic concepts obsolete, making mass education vital for survival, and no education really sufficient to grasp tomorrow's information.

For these and many other reasons, alienation from traditional values and moral codes began. The idea that a person's life should revolve around maintaining the establishment's sleek facade, no matter what maggot-ridden material lies underneath, is quite widely breaking down. New attitudes are cutting across many of society's dividing lines and are based on a new rejection of hypocrisy and the double standard. There is little doubt that the idea of being a single parent very much relates to these changing perceptions of morality.

As one psychiatrist said to me, "What's so unusual about being a single parent, really? People have always separated parenthood from marriage . . . how many women have gotten married or stayed married only because they wanted to be a mother? The only difference now is that they're being honest about it!"

The ability for a woman to be "honest about it" seems unquestionably part of another major force in contemporary life —the evolution of woman as a separate person, seeking her identity through many other channels than the one called marriage.

The organized discontent of women's liberation groups has to some extent heightened the consciousness of all women. It meant the final shove to the already slipping perch of marriage as a woman's only definition, and indeed to marriage as the institution we have known it to be. For while this part of the discussion is centered on the changing self-concept of women, the change inevitably affects a man's view of *him*self, and so also affects the relationships men and women will make with each other.

Even people who would like to cling to yesterday's romantic dream of bride and groom till death do them part, have difficulty ignoring today's untender truth. Our attitudes toward marriage have significantly shifted. Out of this shift come changes in our cultural shape, for at the root of any culture are its attitudes about marriage and family.

The single parents have lifted parenthood out of the institutionalized framework of marriage. To understand their motivation, it seems necessary to take a look at the institution of marriage.

What has it really been like, and what is it like today, and is it possible to predict what it is likely to become?

Actually, it is not that contemporary women are bringing new problems to the marriage relationship, but rather that they refuse to put up with the old ones; those problems that their mothers accepted as a matter of marital course. The unflinching stoicism tied on with aprons, and worn through countless washings of regret came from women who felt that marriage defined them as people. If you believe this, then maintaining the marriage becomes your primary goal and function in life. Not only women but men, too, shared this idea that family stability mattered most of all. The relationships entered "till death do us part" often parted people emotionally long before death made its claim, but there was comfort in knowing the goal of stability was being fulfilled.

When, however, personal happiness and not cultural stability becomes a primary goal, the evaluation of marriage is a different matter. The death of modern marriages in epidemic proportions (there are actually areas in the country that have reported marriage "deficits," where the number of people getting divorces during a particular period is higher than the number getting married!) clearly indicates that happiness, not stability, is what people are after once the honeymoon is over.

One of the interesting side statistics in our ever-escalating divorce rate is that more and more marriages are breaking up after fifteen to twenty years of ostensible contentment. Experts feel that these marriages probably had been unhappy for years, but that at the age of forty-five or so, the impetus to break out instead of "sticking it out" becomes particularly urgent.

The single parent life-style perhaps has its roots most deeply planted in the soil of unfilled promises. Many single parents as children were raised in marriages that seemed to them loveless and unfulfilling. Their early observations made the promise that marriage would bring happiness into their own lives a hard one to believe. They had grown up realizing that the isolation of the "nuclear family," the model of American family life, often contains much more enmity than intimacy. This seems to be why they are generally so dedicated to expanding the concept of family beyond its old tightly patrolled borders.

Whether or not they sympathize with the idea of parents without marriage, most sociologists and psychologists do feel the marriage model itself must change. It must begin to meet the needs of people who have new perceptions of themselves and of the marriage relationship. If marriage and family is to have any viability in the future, it has to free its partners from parasitic dependency, from joyless ritual, from isolating restrictions, and from automatic rather than worked for "rewards."

Traditional marriage has sometimes meant all these things. In its well-oiled machinery it has stifled individuality, leading one psychiatrist to call marriage itself "the great substitute." By this he means that many people and, again, in particular women, have used marriage as a substitute for their personal growth.

Life involves challenge and risk taking, and the grim discontent of many women in their later years (discontent that is often aimed venomously at their husbands) really may stem from self-hatred. They are tormented with the awful awareness that fear of independence led them to make a dependent relationship that choked off their personal identities. Through the years they gave back to their husbands the images their husbands wanted to see, and now when they look in their own mirrors, they see a stranger. Identity crises are common among middle-aged women, and it has less to do with menopause and "empty nests" than it does with the terrible knowledge that they have spent a lifetime in separation from themselves.

There is particular social significance in the female single parent asserting her independence. She is saying that she does not have to depend on anyone else to assume the responsibility of raising a child. The old idea of women as passive and dependent, with hungry needs for emotional intimacy would never have allowed this self-concept. Even now, some women will defend their refusal to move out of the old design with such fluttery arguments as, "I'd much rather be really close to my husband than so tough and independent." Or, "They can have their independence, I like being taken care of." There is a peculiar sort of connotation these women put on the word "independence," as if it were some harsh expletive. They invariably connect it with words such as *hard* and *tough,* seeing an independent woman as someone with no desire for intimate love relationships. Yet when I questioned several psychiatrists, male and female, there was general agreement that a really *dependent* woman can never achieve true intimacy in her marriage.

"Sure, they're cuddly and need taking care of," one physician said. "That's cute when you're ten, but not when you're forty. Believe me, I've seen enough men who are sick to death of carrying their wives' psyches around for twenty years. Nobody wants the responsibility for another person's identity. It may make him feel strong and powerful for a while, but pretty soon it's just a miserable burden." The doctor explained how a woman's "sweet" dependencies can cause her to seriously cut off her husband's freedom, and certainly limits the possibility that he will deal with her openly and honestly.

"Look, if a guy goes off on a business trip, and sees a concert or something one night that he really enjoys, it's natural to want to come home and tell his wife about it. The ability to share in each other's experiences is very much a part of intimacy. But," he said then, "if his wife's going to be threatened that he was capable of enjoying himself without her, he's obviously going to keep the experience to himself, and that is *not* intimacy."

It is instead the spiraling deceit of withheld information and false declarations of feeling that steadily separates people from each other.

The single parent often speaks of the limitations to personal growth imposed by many marriages. The precut patterns of marriage can keep people from experimenting with any new designs. In the name of responsibility and commitment, they will not make certain kinds of decisions or open their lives up to a possible change in direction.

Revolution has been defined as a natural outgrowth of evolution. If this definition is accepted, then we are certainly a society in revolt. So then, too, we must be open to the idea of change in even our most hallowed institutions. The institutions of a society, after all, should prepare its members to exist in the society. Marriage that does not allow for growth and revolt is not fulfilling that function. In a world so filled with turmoil, the old idea that marriage was good when it caused people to "settle down" seems totally inappropriate. This is not a time when anyone can afford to burrow into quiet hiding places or move by a set of unquestioned rules.

People who study contemporary marriage feel that more and more women are frustrated by an image of themselves as narrowly home-centered. They feel, too, that the choice *not* to marry relates to the rising awareness that in marriage there must be room for two independent people of multiple interests. Many single parents see this relationship. "I'm not arbitrarily against marriage," one single mother said. "I just don't want to walk docilely behind someone the rest of my life, stepping in his footprints. When I meet someone I can feel full participation with, I'll probably marry him. But even if I had a child while I was married, I'd see being a parent as a shared, but still independent, experience. So if I feel that kind of independence, then I can have a child outside of marriage!"

When marriage does take place, it is being reshaped in the clay of contemporary experiencing. It is, after all, a human invention, and will therefore change as human beings change.

The major change that confronts marriage is that many people no longer feel they need it, and certainly do not need it in its old forms. Among the dusty old ideas that are being cleared out of tradition's attic, is the idea that there is only one way to live as a family.

Some people will probably go on to reject the idea of family entirely, choosing to live in total independence. Other people will live in groups. Homosexuals will live together and live without apology as homosexuals. Some marriages will encompass outside sexual relationships, other marriages will choose monogamy. Some marriages will last a lifetime, others will be for particular stages of life. Social theorists say that if marriage is to survive at all, it must be open to this kind of freewheeling interpretation of its possibilities. In a world that has such a variety of value systems, it is absurd to think we can continue to declare only one pattern of living legitimate, particularly when so much evidence exists that the pattern is so far from perfect. We have therefore begun to de-mystify the family, have taken off its saintly robes, and are beginning to see it in realistic perspective. It is this hard-eyed perspective that encourages the growth of the single parent family. A man who began a commune with his wife at a point when their marriage was disintegrating said that people choose alternative life-styles largely because the traditional way has stopped working for them.

"You don't look for change if you're satisfied with the way things are. But neither do you keep stoking a fire that's been burned out for months. You take a match and some wood and you begin again."

Obviously the single parent life-style is a way of beginning again. Obviously, too, when we begin, we do not have precedent to fall back on. There is a certain amount of confusion and turmoil in beginnings, but there is also, for many of its participants, great excitement.

One woman psychiatrist speaks enthusiastically about the idea of single parenthood. She welcomes the attempts to unlock people from cultural stereotypes they are supposed to follow either as "feminine" or "masculine" or as a "couple."

This same doctor feels that children of single parents may have the opportunity to stay clear of such rigid classifications of themselves, because they will have grown up against a broadened horizon. "Don't forget," she says, "the single parent, almost by definition has established her own independent identity. Her child should be able to feel he can discover himself the same way without getting locked into 'safe' frameworks or other people's frames of reference."

This particular doctor felt marriage was an anachronism in today's world, but actually not all single parents agree with her. Many would like to marry. It does the single parent experience an injustice to consider it primarily as a rebellion against convention. What the single parent *is* doing is asking new kinds of questions, and coming to different kinds of conclusions. True, they say, they have not married, but this does not mean they cannot be parents.

Dr. Benjamin Spock recently said in an interview that the greatest tool a person can have in times like ours is to be able to deal with freedom. How well single parents equip their children with such tools undoubtedly relates to how they handle their own experiments with freedom. In these pages we will begin to find out.

The Importance of Being Honest

ADOPTION AGENCIES throughout the country report a steady, if admittedly small, rise in the number of children who are returned for adoption some time after the natural, unwed mother has made a decision to keep the child herself. A family service agency in New Jersey reported four such children returned over a one-year period. A ten-month-old, a two-and-one-half-year-old, a three-year-old, and a two-year-old had been brought back to the agency by mothers who discovered they were unable to live as single parents.

For every woman actually able to carry out this dramatic reversal, several others will toy with the idea and go to agencies for advice and counseling. It is reasonable to assume that for every person who does *this,* there are still others who would like to, but are too afraid or guilty to admit their ambivalence just yet.

Psychological experience unequivocally proves that it is far worse to give an older child up for adoption than to do so when he is first born. For now he will suffer from feelings of abandonment, confusion about his worth, grieving for his natural mother and home, and a host of other profoundly painful emotional responses. Also, the decision to give a child up after making an attempt to raise him on her own suggests there was significant stress in the mother's life. It is unlikely that a child living in the circle of that stress would come out untouched. So even before the actual parting of mother and child, the smooth skin of childhood will have shown some quite ugly psychological bruises. The director of a large New England adoption agency was quoted as saying that for reasons of this kind, while he would not arbitrarily discourage a pregnant girl from keeping her child, "the first two years are critical, and if they are damaging years, well, I'm worried about some of the kids who will have to be adopted after all."

Famous personalities such as Vanessa Redgrave, the actress, and Bernadette Devlin, the Irish civil rights leader, smilingly publicize their pregnancies. Soon we read that they are mothers and plan to raise their children on their own; and there is no suggestion of apology to society for the decision. The media's attention to their nonconventional message is in fact one of the influences on the entire culture's rethinking of conventional morality. We tend to associate terrible consequences with violations of moral codes. When smiles instead of tears turn out to be on the "sinner's" face, some of the morality's power over our own behavior begins to weaken. For this, and many other reasons, countless women whose names ring no public bells are deciding they, too, need no wedding bells to keep and raise a child. In the past twenty years illegitimate births have jumped from being one-fifth to one-third of the newborn population. In Boston alone, 45 percent of single mothers are keeping their children compared to 10 percent only ten years ago. In Montreal the percentage has gone up in five years from 20 percent to a rather startling 55 percent.

Adoption agencies are changing their emphasis from adoption counseling to an expansion of services for the unwed mother who is debating whether or not to keep her child. And those bulwarks of benevolent support for society's deviants, the homes for unwed mothers, are all but going out of business for lack of clientele. For *deviant* is still another word hard to confine to yesterday's simple definitions. And it is a word fewer girls today will willingly apply to themselves. Girls who once humbly accepted such cultural labeling, and sneaked off in frightened anonymity to a maternity home, today summarily reject the labeling, openly admit their condition, and stay right where they are—in their own neighborhoods, using family doctors and local hospitals, with business going on as usual right up until their babies' births.

A relationship is made in most earlier research into "illegitimacy" (a word you hardly hear in professional circles today) between the pregnancy and the girl's own relationship with her parents. The pregnancy may be seen, for example, as an unconscious act of rebellion against a domineering mother who has never allowed the girl to discover herself as a woman. Or it could be a way of seeking love from the mother by trying to give her the baby as a symbolic love offering.

Lois, a woman in her late thirties, told a bitter story that was spun from such a premise. Her father had died when she was very young, and Lois always felt her widowed mother resented the extra responsibility of having a small child. Because her mother always had to work, Lois was a latchkey child from kindergarten on. Where other children wore shiny necklaces, Lois wore the metal key hanging from a heavy string around her neck. Every day after school, she would let herself into an empty apartment where she would wait alone until dinnertime. And even then the wait brought little reward, for her mother was as remote as Lois was hungry for open displays of affection.

When Lois was in her early teens, her mother remarried. Soon after the marriage she became pregnant and gave birth to a son. All the warmth Lois was denied was lavished on this child. In fact, the only time Lois really felt close to her mother was when they were sharing some aspect of her brother's care. When the baby was less than a year old, and while Lois was baby-sitting for him, he choked to death on a toy he kept in his crib. Ostensibly he had been asleep; it was a toy he had in his crib every night and was put there by his mother, but nonetheless the burden of guilt was on Lois, in her mind and, she was sure, in her mother's.

A few months later, barely seventeen years old, Lois was pregnant. Up until the accident she had been a virgin. Now she was wildly promiscuous, delighting her high school boyfriends with always available sex in the back seats of their fathers' cars. Not until many years later did Lois realize that she was trying to become pregnant, and the reason why she was trying. Her fantasy had been to "give her mother back her son," and, of course, in doing so to get back whatever scanty portion of her mother's love she had owned before the baby died. As most fantasies do, this one had little resemblance to what happened in reality.

By the time Lois broke the news to her mother, it was too late to have a safe abortion, particularly since these were days when abortion was illegal and in the hands of people of questionable skill. Lois refused to name the father of her child. In fact, she would not have been able to, as there had been a succession of boys in her attempt to conceive. The decision was made to keep the baby, and although Lois felt her mother's tangible contempt, she was convinced it would be replaced by love when the baby was born. Love did enter the house, but it belonged again to the infant, and not to Lois. Her mother took entire charge of the baby's care, making it clear that Lois's irresponsibility and immorality made her unfit to care for him.

Finally Lois moved away from home. She had only intermittent contact with her son, and eventually abandoned the relationship entirely. She is haunted by guilt over the situation. Should she have tried to take him back? Should she be making contact with him now? Despite rather successful therapy, a permanent scar covers a portion of her life, and she says that "there isn't one day of my life that I don't think of him and whether I did or am doing the right thing."

In other traditional views of the unmarried mother, a pregnancy is often seen as relating to the girl's relationship with her father. Many girls, it was felt, become pregnant out of unresolved Oedipal conflict, so that their baby unconsciously becomes, to them, their father's child.

Whether the recipient of neurotic fixation was a mother or father, the major point in this view of unmarried pregnancy is that the girl who "finds" herself pregnant is at least unconsciously not terribly surprised; in fact, statistics often showed that a vast number of girls conceived after having intercourse only once. And as one adoption counselor said, "When you work with the other end of the spectrum, with people who are trying to conceive and can't, you realize what the odds are against this happening only by chance." It does seem that even the most determined skeptic of psychological theory would have a tough time explaining how so many girls got themselves in the right position, at exactly the right time, to become pregnant.

Social changes have occurred so rapidly that over-simplified diagnoses belong in outmoded psychology textbooks. And while this chapter deals with the neurotic distortions of the urge to be a parent, we have to appraise the neurosis in light of society as it is now. Yesterday's easy judgment of pathology has to be held back a bit in the light of what is today's acceptable behavior.

To begin with, the "acting out" aspects of being single and pregnant does not carry nearly the punch it did in the past. Up until ten years or so ago, the "worst" thing a girl could do was come home to mommy and daddy pregnant. My own college memories are filled with hysterical bathroom conversations about whose period was late and what methods did anyone know to "bring it on!" Hot showers, cold showers, alcohol, even someone's bootleg pills from a third cousin who was a cooperative young intern. Girls who were the epitome of sophistication and self-reliance crumbled like frightened children as the marked dates on their calendars passed by.

Today this is pretty pallid stuff when compared to other possibilities of conflict between parents and daughters. A girl who wants to reach a mother or father can do something far more imaginative than becoming pregnant. She can enter into a continuing series of "meaningful relationships," for example, or drop out of school and take a pad in the East Village, or, of course, get really heavily into the drug scene.

While the idea of single parenthood is still startling today, the idea that unmarried men and women engage in the kind of activity that causes people to *become* parents is fairly widely accepted. The age for sexual contact continues to lower, with many studies showing boys and girls in their very early teens are already "experienced," to use one of the older generation's favorite euphemisms.

We must view today's unmarried pregnant girl against a backdrop of social realities that are far more flexible than they have ever been before. For example, we have to realize that when more unmarried people have sexual contact, there are bound to be more slipups and miscalculations that really *can* result in a truly accidental pregnancy. The most foolproof method of contraception, after all, is still abstinence and, barring a medical problem, the best route to fertility is still greater sexual activity. Anyone who remembers the New York City power failure a few years ago may recall that the birth rate rose significantly nine months later. Enough people had the same idea about how to pass the time until the lights came back on so that a good percentage ended up as parents. While we know how they were all acting that long dark night, we cannot conclude that they were all unconsciously acting out particularly neurotic needs!

On the other hand, we should dismiss the temptation to completely ignore psychological history. Even in our revolutionary present, much of the past's behavioral theory stays relevant. The possibility still exists that the decision to become a single parent will stem from neurotic and confused motivations. So the maverick member of the social sciences and not just their stuffier colleagues warn people to consider carefully their reasons for wanting the role of single parent.

One of the problems of our more relaxed social climate is that it allows people to act in ways they might not be emotionally ready for. Evidence shows, for example, that men and women are not necessarily better adjusted than their chaste ancestors just because they have broken free of sexual constraints. If rigid codes once inhibited sensual pleasure, sexual freedom brings its own problems. Overindulgence in the shiny new sexual candy stores can bring attacks of confusion, frightening lack of commitment, and can cause quite serious depression. Studies of the "swinging singles" in various large cities indicate that much psychic pain is coming out of misusing the same freedoms that ostensibly were going to bring happiness. One New York psychiatrist commented angrily that "the pill is the worst thing that's happened to this town." His theory was that because girls no longer had to consider whether a bedmate would be a potentially good husband or father, they drifted into liasons that were transitory and meaningless and were often also emotionally destructive.

In the same way, liberating parenthood from its traditional link to marriage will lead some people who should never take on the experience to the life of a single parent. Various contemporary pressures, however, urge them along. Adoption agencies say, for example, that a great deal of peer pressure can exist for a pregnant girl to keep her baby. If abortions are legal, and parents will finance them, then the antiestablishment move is not to have the abortion but to keep the baby. Friends of the pregnant girl will promise all kinds of physical and emotional support in grandiose fantasies of extended family relationships. But when she takes her baby home to a tiny apartment furnished with the enthusiastic symbols of group involvement—this one's chair, that one's mattress—she may soon find that the furniture stays oppressively empty. The grand group gesture against their parents' value system now over, the friends move on to other interests. And the new mother who has frequently lost her parents' support by her decision is now totally alone.

As I indicated earlier in the chapter, such a confrontation with reality sometimes results in the baby going back for adoption. The longer it takes for this turnabout to take place, the more problems the baby is likely to have. Infants only a few weeks old will show the effects of psychic trauma when denied the emotional security that comes from steady evidence of love and protection. We may live in a time of easy divorce between consenting adults, but divorcing a child from his mother is an entirely different life-game. Separation anxiety is a profoundly deep wound for a child, from which some children never recover. The single parent who is unaware of the extent of her commitment is committing a very, very serious act against another human being.

Very often it turns out that the baby's well-being is not really involved at all in the decision to be a single parent. I was introduced through one adoption agency to a girl named Jeanette, who was considered to be the classic case of ill-considered motherhood. Jeanette was part of the tradition of girls who become pregnant out of conflict with their own mothers. It was, in fact, her mother's decision to keep the baby, saying she would take over the major responsibility of his care. This, by the way, is not an untypical response of many mothers of pregnant girls. For control reasons, for vicarious sexual identification, for their own need to be depended on and feel important as grandma, a surprising number, even when they are ostensibly outraged by their daughter's condition, will openly encourage the girl to keep her child.

In Jeanette's case her mother, true to her word, totally took over her grandson's care. Meanwhile, Jeanette drifted from job to job, unable to really commit herself to any long-term goal. She would come home at night and eat the dinner her mother had prepared for her, and sometimes days would pass before she would see her baby for more than a few minutes. Her mother, though, was obviously happier than she had been for some time, and their own relationship was a good deal smoother than it had been at any other time in Jeanette's life.

After about six months, however, the grandmother had to go on an extended trip. Jeanette was panicky about assuming responsibility for her son, whom she had hardly so much as diapered. She was also, unconsciously, enormously angry at her mother for "abandoning" her. After a couple of particularly bad days, she packed the baby up and went to visit a family service agency someone had told her about. Her intention was literally to hand him over right then and there. Of course, the agency let her know this was not possible, but encouraged her to come for counseling. After several sessions, she was still insisting she wanted to give the baby up. The agency was equally insistent that she take at least another month to consider her decision.

It was a rough month, with the girl calling her counselor nearly daily, spilling over with chaotic confusion. No one was surprised when, one month later to the day, the baby was brought back to the agency door. Shortly thereafter he was placed in a foster home. Jeanette, with the kind of emotional blocking out many girls in these situations are at least superficially good at, found a job and lived by herself in her mother's house, waiting to tell the older woman the news when she returned.

By every indication, the homecoming was violently explosive. Jeanette was literally locked out of the house and told not to return unless she had the baby with her. Her mother would not answer phone calls or letters while, frightened but defiant, Jeannette camped out at various people's homes. It didn't take long for her to capitulate, and she went back to the agency to ask for her baby. The staff tried vainly to dissuade her from acting out of such emotional pressure, but with every attempt to block her, she became more insistent.

The baby was taken away from his foster home and returned to his grandmother, with Jeanette now eligible to assume the role of daughter again.

The agency prevailed on Jeanette to continue counseling. During the sessions, she began to have some awareness of the real dynamics of her situation. Her awareness was stirred, too, by the baby's behavior. Snatched back and forth like some human pawn, he had begun to have such severe nightmares that he was put on a continuing regime of tranquilizers. Faced with the sad clarity of the child's suffering, Jeanette began to see the part she had played in making him suffer. At a terrible price already paid, Jeanette realized that her distorted responses to being a mother were seriously damaging the child she was mother to. As a matter of fact, the counselor said, "It was only at this point that she really perceived that relationship as mother and son. Up until that moment, she had never really seen the baby as a separate person who could be damaged by abuse of his own needs."

The counselor recalled that Jeanette never really had any feeling for the baby at all, except as a tool to use in battle with his grandmother.

With her new awareness, Jeanette made the decision to leave home and place the baby up for adoption. She did not feel capable of raising him herself, now that she realized why she had really had him in the first place. Whether out of lingering needs to punish her mother, or out of real regard for her son, she refused to allow the older woman to have custody. So the baby, still another time, was taken from one environment to another. Newly familiar faces were replaced again with strange ones. The child's rigid body as he was handed over to the agency supervisor clearly showed that another layer of pain had been laid over his abused psyche.

Sadly, no one involved felt they could remedy the situation or come up with a solution that promised the boy more hope for a decent future. One of the terrible aspects of the story of single parents who do not come to honest terms with being a parent is that eventual solutions are, at best, patchwork jobs. They can only try to make the best out of what are already bad life situations.

Awful as this story is, it is better than some others. For ultimately Jeanette was able to see the damage her neurotic interpretation of motherhood had brought to her baby. Many single natural mothers are never able to do this. They become pregnant and are convinced they want only to keep their baby, welcoming the providential "accident" as if it were a joyous gift from God. They live through their pregnancies never really facing the realities of what being a single parent can mean.

And it can mean a great deal of very real stress. Obviously it is easier to share raising a child than to do it on your own. From sitting up at night with a sick baby to handling a school problem, guiding a child through all the troubles and fears of childhood without feeling totally responsible for his failures, or demanding too much in the way of his success (to prove your own success as a parent)—all of these experiences are easier when shared. The effort and the responsibility is so much less overwhelmingly your own. Single parents, unless they have made a real commitment to the extended family life-style, are the primary shapers of their children's lives, and of their adjustments to those lives. A person needs a tremendous amount of ego strength to carry this role off.

It seems that many people who do not have such strength are attracted to the single parent life-style. Instead, they are people who, according to one psychologist, "look to being a parent as a way of getting something instead of as a way of giving something." When asked what that something was, he answered, "Love, of course . . . in the name of which people have made pathological relationships down through history!"

One of the particular signs of a neurotic motivation for being a single parent is the inability to really see a baby as a separate person. Often, in fact, like the unwed mother who is always thought of in those terms, rather than as a parent, the baby of a single parent is often mentally and emotionally conceptualized only *as* a baby. The fact that babies become children very quickly, and eventually autonomous young adults, is another reality rationalized away and, as Scarlet O'Hara said, to be thought about tomorrow. Because it is only the baby who fulfills all the fantasies. It is the baby's dependency that feeds the parent's hunger for love and security. And so it is only a baby she can visualize living with.

Adoption agencies are alert to this particular distortion when they consider a single parent adoption; just as they are when counseling a natural mother about whether or not to keep her child. An adult who is starved for love, who is unable to make successful emotional commitments to independent adults, may invest a baby with the responsibility of being the one source of emotional satisfaction. Such an adult will lock the baby into a circle of "blissful" intimacy, with the parent, of course, always at the center of the circle.

But what happens when that baby begins to strain from the circle, feeling the restrictions, loving as they are? What happens when the baby begins, at around two years old, to say no to commands, or to sometimes prefer the company of other children to his mother? Children at this age are normally involved with finding ways to rid themselves of the dependence that locks them into childhood, that inhibits the necessary moving away that must be done if they are to move ahead to successful adulthood.

"It's quite simple," one psychiatrist said tersely. "Parents who need a child dependent on them to feel loved will not be able to cope with the toddler period."

The story of Elaine reflects this need, and the problems that such needs can bring. The man who made her pregnant had never made any promises of permanency in their relationship. Appropriately for his rather rootless personality, he was an airline pilot. However, his home base was the city Elaine lived in, which meant that she saw him more than anyone else did. But the knowledge that there were other people whom he *did* see when he flew into other cities tormented her. Finally she reached a point where the awareness of where he had come from was spoiling her ability to enjoy him when he came to her. Even though she knew it was absolutely the wrong thing to do, she badgered him for declarations of loyalty, wept about his lack of feeling, and sang all the dissonant songs of love's neurotic needs.

A man like Jim was absolutely the wrong person for Elaine to have become involved with. With the creative ingenuity of the masochist, she had found a man who could stoke the fires of her life-long fear of being abandoned. As she watched her fear come closer to reality because of her tears and recriminations, she decided to have his baby. She told herself that, loving Jim as she did, it was a way for her to always have a part of him. She told herself that she really wanted to be a mother, to give a baby the love she had been denied by her cold, self-involved parents. She told herself, in short, all the folktales of rationalized motives, with the real story left carefully unread.

"Bravely," she never told Jim of her pregnancy. By the time it was confirmed, he was already out of her life. During her pregnancy she planned every single step of becoming a single parent. She fixed up her apartment to accommodate a baby. She took refresher courses in Spanish, for she had been offered a good job as a translator in a publishing house she once worked for. She implied, without really saying so, that she had had a brief unhappy marriage and assured her boss that she would return to work almost immediately after her baby was born. She found a young college student in her neighborhood to agree to a baby-sitting plan that was extremely flexible. Out of the most complex unconscious needs, she made becoming a single parent unusually uncomplicated. With well-oiled precision, the machinery of her life as a single parent was set in motion. Its regular rhythms beat solely for her baby, and old friends marveled at how "natural" a mother she was, although they occasionally commented that she seemed to have "gone overboard." Unless they came to see her, they would rarely get together, for she was reluctant to leave the baby in the evening.

This lovely story of mother love has a "surprise" ending that is perhaps psychologically predictable. When her son was about two years old, Elaine came to visit a psychologist, weeping and in a clear state of panic. She explained that she suddenly found herself being extremely punitive to her child, to the point where she was afraid she might really abuse him. She came for treatment because she was simply overwhelmed at the extent of her anger. For two years she had showered the baby with love, had thought of no one but him, and suddenly, she said, she felt as though she "hated him." After her attacks of rage, she would sink into terrible depression, her guilt as all-encompassing as the fury that had caused it.

Through extensive therapy, she was made to see that the loneliness she had always suffered from was reactivated by her child's growing independence. For his first two years of life, when his extreme dependence was symbolic proof of love, the loneliness had been quieted. But now that it had emerged again, her anger grew from feeling it was "the baby's fault." Simply by growing up he was no longer fulfilling his role, which was to keep the loneliness quieted.

Although at the beginning of her therapy she kept protesting about how much she had done for her son, Elaine was helped to see that her devotion had little to do with any of his real needs. He would have managed without a closet filled with hand-sewn baby clothes. He could have slept without her sleeping in a bed alongside his crib, the better to hear him "the minute he cried." He could have survived the occasional baby-sitting arrangements instead of her almost total abandonment of a social life.

Her therapist explained to me that although Elaine really did love her son, the driving demands of her own hungers dominated their relationship. Her neurotic needs blinded her to recognizing *his* needs, and therefore limited his chance for future emotional health. Much of a child's learning has to do with reinforcement of his behavior by approval or delight or encouragement from his parents. The mother who claps her hands in pleasure when her child takes his first tentative steps toward independence is telling the child it is safe to take those steps. A mother who is threatened by her child's moving away will, by her own fears, make the child feel it is not at all safe "out there." The unknown becomes something to be afraid of. And by not attempting to explore the unknown he can never learn if he can, in fact, handle it.

But Elaine built up no such basis for self-confidence in her son. She was violently upset at his attempts to abandon babyhood. They were signs that he was abandoning her, just as Jim, and her parents, and so many others, had already done. She embodied her two-year-old son with the ghosts of past adult love figures, and the burden of their weight was already crushing his spirit. He was becoming tense and fearful and clinging to his mother. He suddenly began crying when she left his sight. Sadly, Elaine's first response was pleasure. "Look how much he still loves me," she gloated, till her therapist helped her see the terrible distortion in such delight.

"She eventually began to deal with him as a separate person," her doctor told me. "Not completely, of course. They'll both have their share of problems for a very long time, but I think she's got enough real interest in the boy for them to make out fairly well."

This is a story with a relatively happy ending. Not all the stories of single parents end that way. And sometimes they are stories that take a much longer time to tell. Problems that result from confronting the child as a separate person can sometimes occur at adolescence for the first time. Particularly if there is a sexual dynamic to the parent's neurosis, a child's emerging sexuality can shake up a previously calm single parent family.

Ruth will tell you that she always "knew" she would have an illegitimate child. She herself was the product of an illegitimate pregnancy, and she says that from the minute her adoptive parents told her this she felt destined to realize what turned out to be a self-fulfilling prophecy. Ruth was a very attractive young girl with bubbling sexuality. "My whole life was involved with those back-seat strategies of nice-girl battle zones. Touch here, but not there, under the blouse, but not under the skirt. I always walked that very fine edge between being promiscuous and not being square." Then her rather straitlaced parents came in one night and found her necking with a boy. They were extremely punitive. Their self-righteous anger upset Ruth dreadfully, and that, along with her sense that an illegitimate pregnancy lay ahead anyway, made her cross over the line and become relatively promiscuous during the next few years.

When she became pregnant in her early twenties, she began to change. She took her parents' disapproval with bowed head, almost seeming to welcome it. And from the moment her son Michael was born, she became truly another person. She totally denied all sexual expression, becoming, according to the psychiatrist she eventually went to see, "squarer than any middle-class wife for a hundred miles around."

Her decision to keep her baby was seen, in therapy, as having a component of retribution to it, paying herself back for her natural mother's, and her own, loose way of life. Raising the child was an unconscious arena in which to act out her new sense of responsibility, with her "pure" adoptive parents sitting center aisle. By being the quintessent parent, she might win back their approval. And actually she did, to a very great degree. All the rituals of the most stultifying family relationships were reenacted by Ruth and her son and her own parents. Sunday suppers, and Friday night dinners, and daily telephone calls, and shared recipes and laundry hints were the stuff of her life. The boy was given every lesson imaginable from musical instruments to horseback riding, with Ruth always at the sidelines watching and smiling.

She had decided that her primary goal was to be his mother. And this was neurotically interpreted by her as meaning she could not contaminate the purity of the role by seeing men in any relationship that did not relate to it. Once Michael's history teacher, with whom she had had several talks at school meetings, asked her to have dinner with him. Her easy response to him froze. She could only mutter something and walk quickly away, back to the sanctified hush of her living room where no living unconnected with motherhood ever took place.

She could not allow Michael to see her as a sexual being, to have him ever see her with a man whose presence might cause the boy to speculate about the extent of their relationship. For this, it unconsciously seemed to her, would be rubbing his face in her own sins—the sins that were causing him to suffer society's disapproval. Actually, society caused Michael little suffering. His problems, and they were growing, came much more from Ruth's repression and sexual confusion.

In being holier than any thou, Ruth locked herself and her son into what her psychiatrist called a folie à deux. He explained that she had decided that in order to raise her son, who was the result of relatively unrestrained sexual activity, she could no longer engage in any such activity. In language more graphic than the textbooks use, he went on to explain that in actual fact, Ruth had traded motherhood for fucking. Except, as neurotic trades often do, this one had a catch. For in not fucking anyone else, she was really fucking her son, smothering him under seductive covers that allowed him no appropriate sexual expression. Additionally he had no models for sexual identification, having never seen his mother in any sexual aspect with an adult male. Oedipal confusion reigned supreme as he moved into adolescence, and his mother felt that heady mixture of guilt and anger toward any sign that her son was developing as a sexual human being. It is a set of emotions common to many single parents who have not been honest about their own feelings.

While Ruth saw independent parenthood as a sort of penance, many other single parents see the life-style as the ultimate act of independence. Independence is in fact a quality most single parents respect and possess. But like every other quality, it can be neurotically distorted. A single parent should honestly ask herself if her eagerness to handle parenthood on her own really takes into consideration the best interest of her child. Two single mothers I talked to not only had refused to marry the fathers of their children, but would not allow them any role in their upbringing. They were both girls who resented the father-dominated life-style of their own childhoods.

"My mother was in total disagreement with my father about how to raise us," Sally, one of these girls, said. "A lot of good it did her, or us, for that matter. What he said, went. Period."

As a single parent, a mother finds no holds barred. Thumbing her nose at male chauvinism, at the traditional "Daddy's home, everybody line up and please him" motif of much American-style family life, she can be the kind of mother she really wants to be. She can be totally single-minded as a single parent, raising the child with only her own ideas, without any outside influence from anybody!

Adoption agencies are always alert for the man or woman who seems to see parenthood as a way of moving into a cloistered little kingdom over which they have ultimate and irrevocable rule. A child in such a situation has little more freedom to move about than a serf, and a serf he really is in this country if his parent's power needs.

Another common, if distorted, reason for keeping a natural illegitimate child is the hope that it will cement relations with the child's father. Sometimes a girl feels that her pregnancy will awaken the man's protective instincts, so that he will decide he "really does want to marry and take care of her after all." Or her brand of fantasy might focus on the months after she has had the child, when she is sure his father will grow to love him, and "want to make a real home for them all."

Helen was absolutely convinced that the father of her new baby would eventually marry her, even though he told her from the beginning of their affair that he would never leave his wife. She continued to find ways to involve him in the baby's life, from calling him when he was even slightly ill to asking him to baby-sit evenings so she could go to a class. It did not take long for him to get fed up, rather than filled with love, and, leaving her a sizable amount of cash, he relocated his "real" family.

His leaving left Helen feeling alone with the child for the first time since the baby's birth six months before. But more importantly, she was alone with the harsh reality that the fantasy was just that—a fantasy. Without seeing any of the dynamics, she almost totally lost interest in the baby, neglecting him physically and, of course, also emotionally. She had always kept him spotless and contented, just in case his father would stop by—the better to enrapture and capture him. Now, with no hope that he would ring the doorbell, she left the baby dirty for hours, feeding him regularly but with impatient thrusts—eager to have it over with and him back in his crib. Although she really did not need the money, she took a full-time job, making highly unsatisfactory baby-sitting arrangements.

Very soon, the baby was having nightmares, stomach upsets, and increasingly frequent crying attacks. All this, instead of arousing her compassion, only filled her with greater distaste and allowed her to pass the responsibility for her distaste to him. He was simply a "difficult baby," she said. He was probably "brain-damaged," as a matter of fact. Probably she would have to "put him away" some day.

At this point, aware and concerned friends urged her to get help, which fortunately she did. However, she was so deeply confused and had really always been so disinterested in the baby for any true "mothering" reason, that after several months of intensive therapy her attitude toward him had not appreciably altered. In fact it had worsened, for now she was resentful as well as unconcerned. Her anger toward the father's leaving was deflected to the child he "left behind." It was almost with grim pleasure that she would talk about how terrible the baby was, and how he would surely turn out to be as "big a bastard" as his father.

She was finally prevailed upon to put the baby into a foster home. And, with a much-overdue stroke of luck for the child, his foster mother turned out to be a remarkably warm and supportive person. After several months of therapy, Helen decided to move to the West Coast to "start again." She told the foster mother that she would like her to adopt her son, a move the woman was considering at the time of this writing. Every effort was made by Helen's counselors to see that she was equipped with the material to make her move to a new life successful. She was given vocational guidance, educational advice, even put on a diet. For it was the shared opinion that she desperately needed a sense of personal identity, which could only be acquired through feeling some personal achievement. She had never really felt secure in her identity and so, unfortunately, like some other single girls who become mothers, she used her baby as a weapon to coerce a man to *give* her an identity—by making her his wife.

Of course, the idea that someone else can give you an identity through a marriage ceremony is a cultural myth, now rapidly fading from the folklore of our lives. But other myths continue, one of which is that all parents, especially mothers, have instinctive feelings of love for their children. The plain truth is that all mothers do not have strong maternal instincts, as all fathers do not instinctively relate to the role of being a father. And growing up, contrary to another myth, is not always the best time of our lives. Childhood is filled with mysteries the child often is not ready to cope with. It is frequently filled with stress, often stress visited upon the child by the particular pattern of his parents' lives. It is generally agreed that no parent can really raise a child without imposing some kind of stress on him. Whether or not the strains of being the child of a single parent in this day and age are any greater than some received in a conventional family structure, no one can really say right now. As Dr. Spock pointed out to me, we will have to wait until these children are grown, maybe another fifteen or twenty years, to make any kind of comprehensive judgment.

But the single parent does have the obligation to recognize that she is in a sense asking her child to pay the price of her experiment with freedom.

Down through history, petulant children have cried, "I didn't ask to be born." This aggrieved cliché has a particular ring of truth for the child of the single parent. They did *not* ask to be born or adopted into this unusual life-style.

There are many definitions of love in our language, but nearly all share one idea. That there must be a true concern for the other person's needs. A single parent who becomes a parent to fulfill her own needs does not have such concern. This does not mean these parents are not capable of loving their children. It does mean that their neurotic drives for personal satisfaction will inhibit healthy expression of their love.

To put it simply, parenthood is at best a difficult role. We need every bit of strength we can get to make it work. The energy for the job does not come from neurotic compulsions. Unhappy, lonely, frustrated people will not be good single parents. Reasonably adjusted, aware, self-confident people have a running start in this revolutionary new life-style.

The Single Parent – Male

RECENTLY A MEDICAL JOURNAL published a report by a psychiatrist telling of a case of false pregnancy. The physical tricks the mind can play on the body are always interesting. But what was really a mind-bender in this story was that the patient, complaining of nausea, abdominal swelling, increased appetite, and a definite feeling of movement in the abdomen was not a woman, but a man.

OK. We are all terribly sophisticated in this year 1973, and psychological jargon rolls quite easily from our tongues. "Transvestite," we murmur; "delusional psychosis." At the very least, "unresolved homosexuality." But it is not quite so simple. In actual fact, this man, while having certain doubts about his heterosexuality, and clearly experiencing a delusion about his ability to have a child, in many other respects seemed sound, functioning, and relatively well-balanced.

Of course, it is obvious he was a very troubled man, and needed help before his troubles intensified. But is it possible that his dramatic behavior says something rather significant to all of us? There is a theory that the neurotic often anticipates the problems of the general population. By his inability to absorb certain pressures, he throws these pressures into sharper focus when his behavior begins to deteriorate.

What particularly interested me about this case was the therapist's view that his patient resembled many female patients who experience false pregnancy, in that he had developed the symptoms because he needed to have them. That is to say, the implications of the idea of having a baby satisfied very deep needs, and only therapy that responded to these total needs would help him give up the idea that he was indeed carrying a child.

And so I put these ideas together. And I ask myself how much of this man's delusion is based on a loneliness, on a need for really intimate love and interaction that many "normal" men might to some degree share. And I wonder how many problems that men experience in the alienating climate of contemporary life might not be soothed if we could rethink the role of father and its place in a man's life.

Certainly that dusty model of family that sent father off to work to "provide," and left mother home all day to "nurture" is rapidly changing shape. I recently met, for example, a young man who stays home to care for his one-year-old son while his wife goes out to work. Ostensibly he is doing research for a Ph.D. thesis, but he admits he is not into it very deeply.

"This isn't a permanent arrangement," he said. "But I just got fed up with teaching assistant fellowships, and quite frankly I don't know what I want to do in the future. Meanwhile Faye really likes her job. And the fact is, for the most part, I like this job."

He was talking of course about running the house, and most of all, about caring for their baby—"nurturing" him, if you will. "I never saw my father for more than an hour or so a day," he said. "He couldn't possibly have related to me the way I do to my son. Intimacy takes a certain amount of time. It doesn't come naturally just because you've supplied the sperm for the kid to develop."

This is a book about single parents, and this a chapter about single fathers, yet the man I just mentioned has all the old credentials for being a father—marriage license, wedding ring, legal approval. I introduced him quite deliberately. For in actual fact, he serves to illustrate how "natural" and legitimate the idea of a man becoming a single parent really is. Social change does not come about by storming the palace steps in mass numbers; it comes from a steady progression of individuals taking small, then bigger, then even bigger steps toward breaking the palace orders. Each step blends into the ones that came before, and widens the path for those who will come along next.

And so the young father, married, who says, "To hell with Sophie Portnoy and 'momism,' men are parents too"; who says he really enjoys being close to and taking care of his baby, has paved the way for what the single male parent now says by his choice of life-style. For the single man who assumes the role of parent, willingly, who in fact seeks it, often surmounting significant obstacles to achieve it, is saying that the old definitions of words such as *support* and *nurture* and, here it comes, *maternal instinct,* do not fit anymore. A new dictionary is called for, and there will be plenty of cross-references in its pages.

All the angry writing from advocates of women's liberation, all the strident talk of motherhood myths and baby traps fade in impact at the simple picture of a man cuddling his child with no wife having to smile benign encouragement at his side, ready to grab the baby before he gets hurt by awkward male attempts at affection. And no stronger argument for eliminating biologic and cultural roles and replacing them with "human" roles exist than in such a picture. For if that hallowed or disputed maternal instinct can be defined at all, it would imply a deep instinct for wanting children, a desire to love them, and cherish, and nurture, and support, and protect them in deeply emotional and not just physical ways. If this is what it means, then the single father is saying, in as clear a voice as we shall ever hear, that if not all women have such feelings, many men do.

If a woman's ability to move from marriage into full independent identity as a single parent has evolved in part from the women's liberation movement many consider to be so historically significant, the male single parent is part of the same evolution. We should bear in mind always that men as well as women have been the victims of rigid sex role definitions of who they could be. If women were locked into mushy dependency by their "emotions," men were locked into such emotional isolation that they seemed destined to stop functioning as emotional persons.

A single father named Steve talks about this. He lives in a small house he built himself at the edge of a woods in New Hampshire. A group of friends, all but one couple married, live in five similar houses forming a kind of compound. Two of the women care for the six children of the group while the men and the other women go out to work. They are paid by the group for their function, and the other adults often participate in special projects with the children that might require more, or more specialized, supervision. In the evenings, or on weekends, each family is on its own, although many, of course, choose to exchange baby-sitting services or take part in activities together. They are, after all, friends, and in a way, the larger family they represent as a whole is only an extension of their smaller, individual units.

"Actually, it's the best of both worlds, I think," Steve said. "I spend a lot of time with Billy as 'just the two of us.' But I also have the security, as does he, of having many other people to trust and help care for him. It's a lot different from the family I knew when I was a child, I can tell you that," he said with a smile.

"But then," he continued, "I suppose that's what having Billy is all about. Obviously if my own family had 'worked' for me, I wouldn't have chosen this kind of model for myself, or more importantly, for Billy."

We were sitting in Steve's combination living-dining-kitchen room built of rough beams and wide-pegged floors. It was a beautiful room. The woods blended with each other, and a fire in the brick fireplace deepened their tones, which kept changing as the outside light went through its own changes. On the walls were some of Steve's paintings. Muted abstract designs with just the hint of a woman's form or a city street. Interspersed with Steve's paintings were some of Billy's—great gobs of color in childishly whimsical shapes. There was little furniture in the room. What there was was built into the walls, so that the room offered a maximum amount of living space. I thought of the homes of some people I know. Their rooms are crammed so full that formality is almost demanded of visitors and make anyone, close friend or family member, feel like a visitor.

But now, here, as Steve and I talked, Billy ran the full length of the room pushing a toy truck in front of him. It was a room that obviously belonged as much to him as it did to his father, and perhaps this is why he was so remarkably able to let Steve and me speak without interruption as we shared its space together.

I talked to Steve about this, and about the whole idea of a thirty-six-year-old man pulling up stakes and starting a new life as a single father. Steve, a teacher, had moved to New Hampshire from another state after Billy's adoption. He had always wanted to live in the country, he said, but "it's a life you should share. Now I have someone to share it with."

Was he implying, as many single parents do, that sharing through marriage wasn't in store for him? Maybe so.

"I haven't met anyone I can see being committed to as a husband. But does this have to mean I can't be a father when that's a commitment I feel very able to fulfill? Maybe I'm simply a person who would make a better parent than I would a husband."

It was a simple statement, but it rang in my head, bouncing from side to side like a ball from some childhood game . . . knocking over assumptions and connections made automatically down through the years. Men not wanting to be husbands, but men who do want to be fathers, and men who see this role as a part of their human experience without upsetting their own sense of themselves *as* men.

Steve is clearly unconcerned about maintaining society's traditions, but he has also to a large degree created his own society. Is this what "counter-culture" really means, I wondered?

He had originally bought this plot of land with one other friend, the husband of the woman who now helps take care of Billy. Together they had built their houses, needing only minimal help from local contractors. The compound grew when distant friends, some curious about Billy, came up to visit, and were smitten with the contrast between their own city lives and Steve's new life-style. There is a theory about social change that says it comes about when new ways of living become "plausible." The more possibilities we see in ways of behaving, the more we can entertain the idea of changing our own behavior. So the people who now share the compound with Steve were admittedly influenced by the idea that this way of life was possible for Steve, and so perhaps for themselves.

In the same way, single fathers grow in number as more men see others take on the role. When the unfamiliar becomes familiar, acceptance increases. Steve felt that adoption agency attitudes were reflecting this change, but said he imagined they were still investigating the potential single father very thoroughly.

"They really put me through the mill," he said with a grin. "You know, the whole 'fag' trip. I practically had to get affidavits from girls saying I'd slept with them and that I was really OK in bed!"

I smiled with him, but I knew I had had this question buried in my own compartmentalized mind. It was a mind, I was discovering, that was well trained to automatically categorize male-female emotional roles, and to quickly judge any man trying to alter those roles. How incredible it is, I thought, that we have so removed men from an emotional life that we immediately assume only an unnaturally "feminine" man could experience deep emotional involvement with a child.

Steve talked about this aspect of being a single father. "You have to be really sure of yourself to make it through this experience. I'll admit to feeling some twinges of fear about the whole machismo bit, when I'm sewing up Billy's pants, or getting him ready for bed. There's an awful lot of inculcation to undo before many men are going to feel comfortable about experiencing themselves in such new ways."

It is true that society has placed the emotional life outside the male experience. In all that is said in these pages and elsewhere about the shifting sex roles, the fact is that men are often the least equipped to deal with the emotional strain caused by changing definitions. As I said before, if women have been locked into their emotional lives, men have been locked out of theirs. And so the threat to his "superiority," the usurping of his traditionally male turf in work, sex, and general behavior may cause a man really severe emotional upheavals. And barren as he has been emotionally he does not have the tools to cope with the complex feelings he may be suddenly facing.

Steve had taken Billy outside to set up a croquet set, and I saw him encouraging the boy next door to play a round. Steve suggested the game when he saw his son staring pensively out of the window. I had only grown conscious that the room was quieter, that the boy had stopped loping back and forth with the tinny-sounding truck. But I certainly had not picked up the signals that caused Steve to gently break the child's reverie and move him outside the house. What he was really doing, of course, was moving the boy outside of himself, out of whatever inner distress had changed his mood from joy to sadness.

Steve later explained that Billy occasionally did become depressed, but that as their relationship continued, these moods were much less frequent. The adoption agency had warned him that taking on an older child often meant such mood swings. After all, the inner life of orphan children is rarely richly fed.

Steve, like other single fathers, found the idea of assuming responsibility for another person's emotional life frightening but also, in a way, the most exciting aspect of the single parent experience.

"To really touch another human being, isn't that what we're

all after? If I can touch Billy's inner world, my own life will be infinitely richer. I really don't want him to grow up part of that whole impersonal, external achievement, powerful male image, trip I was part of."

More and more men are questioning these traditional measures of their lives. New focus for living is being demanded, and a surprising number of men are making attempts to find that focus. While women's liberation activities receive a great deal of our attention, it is less well-known that numerous men's consciousness groups are springing up throughout the country.

Another single father, Gary, feels his decision to adopt his son was totally a result of the strength he received from his men's group. "A strength that was real, real enough to say I didn't have to live out the old definition of 'strong.' Five years ago, I wouldn't have been caught dead being demonstrative to a child the way I am with Mike."

Much of men's consciousness-raising has to do with a man's inability to reveal himself on any feeling level. Group members become newly aware of how they perceive others, and particularly other men, as competitors, which makes any real openness impossible. The men in Gary's group quickly saw how aggressive they were with each other, how on guard against "being taken advantage of," how little they listened to anyone else in their need to "be the one with the answers." Intrinsic to this behavior are our attitudes toward homosexuality. As I shall discuss more fully in the chapter on homosexuality, the fear of being considered homosexual plays a tremendously important part in a man's behavior. If you don't cling fast to sex role definitions of who you are, won't you be opening the door for homosexual labeling and, worse, perhaps even some repressed bisexual feelings?

One of the major changes in life today is the questioning of just how "abnormal" bisexuality really is. There are actually many professionals who feel people are naturally bi- rather than heterosexual, and it is only society's decision that one is "bad" that has made us reject it as a plausible life-style.

Whatever the truth of this question, the fact remains that far too many men have starved themselves emotionally, and abused themselves psychically and physically to prove their masculinity. They look for their identity in their sexually defined "role." If a man is a man when he is "tough," then he must keep toughness at the center of his being—must fight and control and step over those in his way in order to define himself in other men's eyes. "Manliness" can become almost a metaphor for all kinds of life patterns. There are those who see even our prolonged stay in Vietnam as relating to this deeply ingrained attitude. It is not "manly" to admit defeat and pull out of a war. Just as it is not manly to admit tenderness, or fear, or to cry, or be gentle. These are the distortions of self that Gary's consciousness group are grappling with. "I think they just asked me in because I was what they most disliked about themselves," he said with a self-deprecating laugh. "You know, your typical male chauvinist pig. Impossibly arrogant, interested only in a woman's body, never in what was inside her, except of course if it was me."

How glib. How slick. How could this man have decided to be an adoptive single father?

Because he felt that the glibness, the slickness, which is still part of his "outside" skin, had shut off learning the real vocabulary of meaningful living. He had always been easily successful. His really remarkable good looks made conquests almost routine. His intelligence and charm made office doors open as welcomingly as the ones to bedrooms.

"But I was like a phantom," he said. "I was totally outside myself, watching myself go through the motions of my life. In the four-o'clock-in-the-morning places of my spirit, I was scared to death. I joined the men's group because I had reached a time in my life when I felt I could relate to no one. No one at all."

Gary also spoke of his childhood, where his father had been passive to the point of almost total noninvolvement. Consequently, Gary had missed the companionship of a male figure. There were two older sisters in the family, but no brothers, or even close male cousins.

"I had lots of friends," he said, "but no one I could really feel close to. And it was very funny, but I consciously felt the lack of such a relationship—another male to be more open with than I could be with my friends. There was just too much peer-type competition among us for that to happen."

Like many single parents, a combination of external events and internal changes precipitated the decision to adopt a child. Gary was promoted to vice-president in the advertising agency where he worked. This meant quite a bit more entertaining than he'd previously been doing, so he decided to hire a housekeeper. Simply by luck he found a really extraordinary woman.

"The only irritation I ever had from her was that she kept 'subtly' suggesting I get married; but she only wanted it so I would have kids. She's absolutely nuts about kids."

And then one day Gary read about a man on the West Coast who had become a single father. "I never remember a feeling like that before," Gary said, "except the first time I visited Paris. A real shock of recognition. I knew when I hit Paris that it belonged to me, because it fit every fantasy I'd ever had. And when I read that story, I knew I would have to adopt a child. It seemed inevitable and natural—a decision I had repressed but would never again question."

Once this awareness exploded in Gary however, he began to have other, much less exciting thoughts, heavily laden with self-doubt and anxiety. He was sure the agency would turn him down. All the questions he had had about himself before joining the men's group surfaced again. Was he all slick facade and nothing underneath? Was he capable of stripping off the patina of his outside self and really relating to anyone else? He was sure the agency people would view him as some dissolute swinger who wanted a child for some new "kick," and who would never have the child's best interest at heart.

"It was awful," he said to me, "I'd go to the damn agency, after, mind you, asking for the appointment myself, wanting to erase the crummy impression I was sure I'd made the last time. Then I'd open my mouth and hear myself sounding just as arrogant and obnoxious as I'd done before."

Obviously, his perceptions were exaggerated, as his friends in the men's group continuously assured him. For, despite his fears, Gary impressed the agency as someone who truly wanted a child, and for legitimate reasons. But it was not a quick decision by any means. His life was investigated with intense thoroughness. As with Steve, they went into his social life and his business life. They talked to his housekeeper and were satisfied that her own desire to participate in the raising of a child stemmed from genuine affection for children and the man she worked for, and not from some unresolved psychological conflict about her own childlessness.

"We weren't being controlling or power mad," the agency counselor said. "After all, there are still many agencies who won't consider the idea of single men as parents. Actually, the fact that we are to some degree pioneers made us feel our responsibility doubly. It would set things back for a lot of people if we allowed an adoption that ended badly."

As for Gary, he told me, "I had the idea I was passing the test for every man who came after me. It made me mad at first, but then I liked the idea. When I got the news that I had finally been accepted, I had this sense I had done something for my 'brothers' . . . the way women talk now about 'sisterhood.' It's a powerful feeling—exciting as hell, and enormously moving."

Shortly after his acceptance as a potential parent, Gary was called down to see the child they had in mind for him. For the most part single parents adopt older children, both out of their own feeling that an infant would be too overwhelming, and because the single parent is still, by and large, not the first priority of adoptive agencies. They tend to get the children other two-parent families do not adopt. An older child, like the handicapped child, is harder to place than a new baby, and therefore becomes a likely candidate for a single parent family.

The first encounter with six-year-old Mike, as Gary describes it, was a dreadful one in every possible way.

"I felt when I saw Mike that my fantasies had been ripped to shreds. Incredible, devastating disappointment—to the pit of my stomach."

Although he had told himself any child Mike's age, orphaned since birth, shunted around from foster home to foster home, would have obvious problems, he could not break through his violently negative response. The boy was too quiet —on the other hand he laughed too loudly. He wasn't nice looking—too skinny. He was small for his age. His hair was straggly.

The agency counselor accompanied Gary and Mike to lunch at that first meeting. The child remained somber and quiet, showing no glimmer of interest in the menu despite its almost overwhelmingly child-oriented possibilities. Hamburger, hot dog, spaghetti, pizza—"It doesn't matter," Mike said.

Chocolate-marshmallow, vanilla-fudge, peppermint-stick ice cream—Mike "didn't care."

"I'm a big ice-cream freak," Gary grinned, when he told me the story. "Crazy as it sounds, in the tension of that day, I jumped on Mike's disinterest in the flavor of ice cream he wanted as the reason I needed to say he wasn't for me. To like everything equally meant you liked nothing at all, had no passion, no imagination. Of course, to a great degree I was really thinking about my own father—that passiveness that always gets me up the wall when I see it now in other people. Noninvolvement that never touches life. I certainly didn't want to involve myself with that kind of kid."

Gary went home that night singing this song in all its dissonant, rationalizing variations. But he woke up in the middle of the night realizing it was a song whose lyrics had been imposed upon Mike's tongue. If the child was passive, then random care had made him so. Who had ever allowed him to assert his own ego? And how could the boy not be afraid of saying the "wrong" thing to a man who might carry his destiny in his hands? Better not to say anything at all. "Here I was," said Gary, "only thinking, did I want this kid or didn't I. I suddenly realized what he must be thinking—what I symbolized to him. On one hand the way out of a life of foster care, on the other hand leaving what was at least familiar for a way of life he had no possible perception of. What an incredible dilemma for him. I lay there in my bed and had this intense feeling of empathy for him, and I knew we had to get together again."

It was arranged the next day for Mike to be brought to Gary's apartment for dinner. Gary did his best not to overwhelm the child, and cautioned his housekeeper to do the same. Slowly Mike seemed to unwind, at least a little. Gary watched him as he fiddled with the huge color TV set, or touched the dials on the stereo set, and a spark of light seemed to flicker behind the dull mask of his eyes.

As I sat in Gary's colorful living room, I could well imagine how unbelievable its treasures must seem to a child whose life had previously held little more than the bare elements for survival. Yet it was extremely dificult to connect the boy I had just met with the one he had been that day. Mike was alert, and charming, and seemed truly at ease. But Gary was still remembering, and now he reached over to touch the arm of the slightly worn, but deeply piled chair I was using.

"You know," he said to me, "it was this chair that really decided me to take him. Mike kept coming over to it that night and stroking it. When we ate, I saw him looking over to it; and just before they were going, he stood near it and made this long swoop with his hand from top to bottom. I knew it must symbolize everything warm and soft and comforting this kid had been deprived of. Again, I had this feeling that I had connected with his pain, and then that I *wanted* to connect with it, so I could help him get rid of it."

And so the decision to adopt Mike was made. There was an interim period of trial for both agency and Gary to see if the decision was a good one. It was a year not without real problems, for the single parent story, after all, is more adventure than fairy tale. As Gary already knew, no child who has lived without steady parental love, who has suffered the small and large despairs of a life like Mike's, could move into a new life without a great deal of heavy psychological baggage.

On the agency's suggestion, Gary and Mike went for counseling, a service offered as part of the agency's multipurpose facilities. This, together with the support of his friends, helped Gary enlarge his own support to the boy, so that he in turn felt safe in opening himself up.

Gary recalled how during those first months Mike seemed to vacillate between unresponsiveness and defiance. Through counseling, Gary was able to see how these rigid poles of behavior gave the child a kind of security. To act more spontaneously to the flow of his new life would require a great deal more sense of self than he had attained.

As for Gary, he admitted to feeling resentful at times, angry at times, overwhelmed at times, and deeply discouraged many, many times. "But I knew I wanted to stick it out. And I knew that if I could manage to do it, it would be good one day."

Was this again an act of male assertion? Was he "proving" his ability to conquer the problems of being a single parent? He said no.

"I wanted Mike in my life. I can't begin to tell you all the reasons why. I needed a reciprocal love relationship. I needed to have a base at the center of my life. I needed to get behind the facade that's become my way of operation in the world. But I wasn't using Mike, and I didn't feel he owed me anything. I just wanted it to work, that's all. I didn't bother to analyze why, and maybe that's the best argument I have for how real my feelings were."

As they continued to explore each other, rather than their own responses, things did begin to become "good." There were several setbacks, as when Gary had to go on a business trip and leave Mike behind. Or when a child in Mike's first grade class (where he was having considerable trouble fitting in) chose Mike to be the victim of his bullying. When Gary's housekeeper told him that Mike was coming home from school breathless every day and locking himself in his bedroom, Gary tried to find out why. It took two weeks of patient, direct and indirect questioning to get to the heart of the boy's severe distress.

"I could tell, when he finally told me the story," Gary said, "that the real problem was he didn't know how I wanted him to respond. Mike's a wiry kid, and I'm sure he wouldn't have been afraid to tangle with just about anyone. Believe me, he had to do a lot of defending himself before he came to live with me. The trouble is," he said thoughtfully, "that he *was* living with me, and he didn't know what I'd want him to do. Do we fight back, or do we back away? He wasn't sure, and he wasn't sure enough of our relationship to discuss it with me."

Gary tried to give Mike the sense that he could make judgments without worrying about losing his own approval; and then tried to give him some guidelines about peer relationships that would allow him self-pride without having to prove his masculinity in the old show-how-tough-you-are way.

When Gary announced his business trip, Mike's behavior took a marked turn for the worse. Gary easily confessed to real feelings of anger toward the child at the time. He had a great deal to do in preparation for the trip, and Mike's demands affected his ability to think clearly.

"I had several times where I really resented him terribly. Times when I doubted my sanity in taking on such a load. But then I realized what was going on. When I understood how frightened of abandonment the kid really was, I was able to talk to him directly and then, in more subtle ways, show him that our relationship wasn't going to be altered by my being away."

Nonetheless, Gary found his travels very different than they were before Mike came into his life. He cut his trip short at the first possible chance, instead of prolonging it as he was apt to do in the past. Yet he tells me this with no regret. He clearly wanted the feeling of someone to come home to, even if the coming home involved some difficult readjustment and soothing of tensions that had piled up during his absence.

The real story is that Gary became increasingly aware of Mike's responses and emotional needs. Their communication moved to deeper levels of experience, to rawer formulations of personal concerns. As their intimacy grew, so did Mike's trust in the man he wanted desperately to love. And if Gary ever doubted his own feeling, it was dispelled as the time for the official adoption to take place, grew near. The stakes had become high for them both, and losing implied a loss that was almost immeasurable.

They did not lose each other. Instead, now officially father and son, they went on to share more and more of their separate lives. It is a life, of course, greatly eased by Gary's financial income. While he is remarkably open to the unglamorous sides of parenthood, he does, in fact, have a remarkable housekeeper, who can share, if not take over, much of the day-to-day work of child care. The other value Mrs. Giles, the housekeeper, provides, is being a continuing female presence in Mike's world. Most psychiatrists agree the single parent should try to bring people of the opposite sex into their child's life. Gary, as a very eligible bachelor, is also able to supply younger women, to supplement the grandmotherly female presence of Mrs. Giles.

Gary is conscious of the confusion he can create in people's minds when they meet him and Mike for the first time. The news that he is not widowed or divorced but a "single parent" can cause some eyebrows to rise. He remains for the most part unperturbed by this.

"I've done that trip already," he says. "A really secure man doesn't have to worry about 'looking' masculine. I don't give a damn what other people think. I know what I think. And I've never been surer about who I am than during these last two years."

Like Steve, Gary remains cool to the idea of marriage. "Sure, it would be nice to share life with another adult," he said. "But most of the time, you find yourself carrying them around instead. Right now, it just isn't in the cards for me. Still, I'm certainly open to the idea that as I continue to change, and as women become surer of themselves, I'll find some woman I can have a mutually interdependent relationship with. What I can't see is living in the traditional marriage model, or myself being the traditional husband."

Gary, too, reflects the ways most people are striving to redefine themselves as people first, whether they are male or female. There is unquestionably a need to find a role balance between the sexes, and within the societal institutions, that will be free from stereotype; that has instead a recognition of each individual *as* an individual. There is a need to respect each person's individual integrity, and his right to choose the particular shape of his life. The single father, who is untying himself from stereotype and opening himself up to new possibilities for life as a man, is perhaps singularly well equipped to father the children who will live in tomorrow's world.

Who Are the Unmarried Mothers of Today?

IN 1944, A WELL-KNOWN ACTRESS named Lupé Valez committed suicide. She was pregnant, and the father of her baby refused to marry her. Miss Valez's tragically simplistic view of her dilemma—she wrote in her suicide note that there "was no other way out"—dramatically illustrates how far we have come from those early days of our lives.

For the single pregnant woman today, there are a variety of ways out. But more importantly, there are a variety of ways for her to stay in the culture's perimeters, even though she has moved outside its traditional value system. Her heretical but heady awareness of independence very much relates to the idea of being a single parent. The fact that a woman can begin to see herself as a self-sufficient person allows her to shake free of an idea even more deeply buried in her consciousness—that she needs a man to depend on in order to raise a child. It is interesting to talk to career women from some twenty years or so ago. Those who married (and many felt the choice was *either* marriage *or* career and so did *not* marry) still felt that once children were involved, the husband was the dominant figure in the family.

"I know that even though I worked all through our marriage," one high school teacher told me, "I had this idea that I needed a man to 'take care' of me and the children. They were incredibly inseparable ideas to me," she says wonderingly. "Here I was, working in a ghetto school, and organizing teachers' unions, but once I became a mother, I believed I had to depend on a man for 'protection.' "

The single mother of today, however, like Elaine, will say that such a belief is a myth. A myth people like herself decided to question.

"Women are certainly capable of supporting themselves emotionally and financially," she says. "The only difference is that society and the woman herself never really believed it. Now women *know* it's true, and are demanding that the culture accept it, too. Look," she says earnestly, "it's *all* folklore. How many men walk out on women after they're married and never give them any financial help? And how many men really support their wives emotionally? Believe me, it's a lot better to rely on yourself. I'd much rather pull my own weight in a relationship than have to worry when the ax is going to fall because my husband decides he's tired of me or loses his job, or even just gets sick."

Elaine has negative feelings about marriage; she is, in fact, against any life-style that smacks of dependency on a man. But I met many single women who would like to marry—either the man who fathered their child, or someone they hope may still appear in their lives. Contrary to the idea that most single mothers are, like Elaine, waving banners of "down with marriage bans," a recent study of unwed mothers showed that six years after their babies' births, 50 percent had married. Of that 50 percent, half had actually married the baby's father. It is true they reversed the "normal" sequence of events, but they ended up with a quite familiar family style.

A range of attitudes toward marriage can also be seen in

women who adopt babies as single parents. Some women, such as Betty, a fifty-year-old English professor, knew from the time they were little girls that they "didn't want to be married, but wanted to have lots of children." It took Betty almost fifty years before the culture made this goal possible, but it was always a goal clearly in mind. Other women, such as Annette, a black Chicago physician, felt differently. She says that even though she always wanted to be a doctor, she wanted equally to be a wife and mother.

"But medical school took up so much of my time. I turned around one day and realized I was almost forty and that I'd concentrated my energies of the last twenty years on getting an education and building a career. After I stopped feeling sorry for myself over that realization, I decided I'd better see about adopting a child. At least I could fulfill the family part of my dream. Who knows," she adds with a smile, "maybe I'll still get the other part, too. The baby makes me feel I'm beginning all over again, so anything is possible!"

As I wrote in the Introduction, it is impossible to offer a composite picture of today's unmarried mother—natural or adoptive. Yet in the past she was only seen in composite caricature. Or at least an unwed natural mother was. (The idea of a single woman adopting a child was an idea itself yet unborn.) Not quite twenty years ago, *Out of Wedlock* by Leontyne Young, a study of unwed mothers was published that did in fact attack some of society's prejudice. Nonetheless, the Introduction painted her picture in sweeping general terms: "The girl was young, in her mid-twenties . . . (with) lines of strain on her face. . . ." it began. And after describing her physically as a person, it went on to describe the culture's attitudes about the person she was. She had run away from home, the book said, "to escape the shock and anger of her family, the whispers of her neighbors, the curiosity and condemnation of the community. . . . Refugees from public criticism, they (unwed mothers) neither expect nor receive understanding from society; and to their already heavy personal problems is added the weight of threatened punishment and enforced secrecy."

Contrast this, if you will, with a recent article by Isadore Rubin entitled "Transition in Sex Values—Implications for the Education of Adolescents." Reporting on a conference of college deans and guidance counselors, the author explained the conference was called because guidance people shared the confusion of the students and parents they were supposed to advise. What, after all, did constitute a valid set of sexual mores? Predictably, the conference ended as it began, with no agreement reached. This analysis of our transitionally elusive value system concluded, "Whether we like it or not, we do not today possess a code of beliefs about which we can agree. . . . Our modern sex morality can no longer consist of laws which give a flat yes or no answer. . . . There are many moral decisions which persons must make for themselves."

This is, of course, what the woman who chooses to be a single parent today is doing. But the reasons for her decision are often very different from those of another single parent. The advantage of a stereotype is that it neatly irons out differences under one fits-any-size labeling. Yet it is really an injustice to the single parent experience not to see how nonhomogeneous a group single parents can be. Like any other behavior, unmarried motherhood has a variety of meanings in the light of a particular person's life.

The report that dealt with the six-year follow-up of unwed mothers firmly told its primarily social service audience that the days of composite labeling must be over. The only thing the study subjects had in common, the authors wrote, was that they had given birth to a child. Short of that, their lives took on as many different patterns as any other group in society.

"There's a big difference," one psychiatrist said, "between the girl who keeps a baby after she becomes pregnant, and a girl who finds some guy to use as a stud so she can conceive. The former may be motivated by very positive feelings of self-sufficiency. The latter can be lashing out at men as a group for making her feel inadequate."

Alice is a nervous, red-haired woman in her late thirties. She has had two children going the "stud" route, a fact she announces the moment you meet either one of her young sons. She has a tendency to hurl her words at a listener, barely pausing to wait for a return. It is an exhausting experience talking to her, because there is a sense of competitiveness—a feeling that if you want to figure in the conversation at all, you will have to fight her to the mat for equal time. Her aggressive statements of self are wearying and cause a kind of instinctive regression to simpler days. There is a sudden urge to take on all the old trappings of femininity—to curl your hair and wear frilly aprons and bake chocolate chip cookies by the dozen, to cancel subscriptions to news magazines, to cry a lot and giggle often.

On the other hand, her fervor is also compelling, and pulls you, if reluctantly, out of yesterday into today. No other single parent I had talked to was so zealously chauvinistic about her life-style. We are not on our way anywhere, she told me. We are already here. This is tomorrow. This *is* the brave new world.

I tried for objectivity as she explained that world to me, and how she came to enter it. The penis and the vagina, she said, are only the necessary parts for conception. There is nothing sacred about the process. Our fairy-tale hypocrisy has made it seem otherwise, but there is no love that matters except between a mother and her children. Perhaps someday when men and women get themselves straightened out, they will learn how to relate to each other as people. But for now, there are years of oppression to make up for and any woman who believes in the future of women must reject men. We cannot have intimate relationships with oppressors. First women have to develop self-pride, self-worth. Men will have to learn to relate to women without struggling to control them. But that is their struggle, and no woman of this generation should waste her energies by helping them as they have too many struggles of their own, imposed by men.

Alice made conceiving a child through sexual intercourse sound like instructions that come in cartons of unassembled furniture. "Place part A inside part B. . . ."

That is her no-nonsense view of things. She is a firm believer in the significance of well-planned environment, feeling herself was a victim of thoughtless, imposed environment. It should be said here that Alice's militancy is much less a result of her membership in various women's liberation groups as it is in her much earlier personal history. She was the only girl in a family of five children, and as a result was fussed over and babied.

"But I was never pretty enough to really make it outside," she says bitterly. "And I had no other tools except to *be* pretty. All my energies were supposed to go toward making some boy like me. When they didn't I felt totally worthless. For all my growing-up years," she says, "I was supposed to be concentrating on how I looked to *other* people, while my brothers were learning who *they* were as people. My entire way of valuing myself came from how boys and men valued me. I had nothing to give myself on my own."

The environment that Alice will now provide for her children will be of her own design, dependent on no man for its creation. In the light of this attitude, her decision to "pick a man, any man" to father her children is reasonable. Yet, a social worker who is quite an independent lady herself, later commented: "You wonder what a woman must feel about herself to use men in this dehumanizing way. It's a form of prostitution, of contempt for herself as well as for the man. I worry about the attitudes she'll impart to her sons about their own self-worth."

And a psychiatrist, who had seen a single mother very much like Alice in therapy, talked about how women like this are "unwilling to be vulnerable." He also worries about this because he believes we have to show vulnerability sometimes, if we're ever to really get close to anyone else. If we constantly keep our guard up, we never let down the masks, and so never feel that anyone has really seen us. "And that's really what she needs," the doctor said, "to feel that the person she really is inside is someone worthy of other people's love. If she never lets anyone see that person, how will she ever experience that kind of feedback? I hope," he said then, "that with her children, she'll at least be able to do this. If not, her life will be as totally unsatisfactory as an aggressor as it was when she felt a victim."

Tama is not as far along the spectrum of social reaction as Alice, but is making a similar statement by her decision to remain a single parent. Tama became a single parent because of her vehement dislike of the power plays found in traditional marriage. She was raised in a Russian Orthodox home by a father who was extremely authoritarian. "With his wife/child as much as with his real children," Tama says wryly. The particular aspect of her parents' relationship that led Tama to the kinds of adult relationships she made was her father's excessive jealousy. Her mother was a beautiful woman, and her father was continuously upset by men paying her any degree of attention.

"In analysis," Tama told me, "I remembered an incident that I'd repressed, but that I'm convinced really changed the course of my life. I was about four years old, and the three of us went on a cruise. My mother and I had gone for a walk around the ship, and a young captain started talking to us. He offered to explain how the ship worked, and we went up front with him. I got bored and was kind of playing around on the floor. My mother was sitting up on a life raft watching while he demonstrated some of the equipment. I can remember it all now so vividly. From where I was on the floor, I could see my mother's white skirt fluttering, and she was swinging her legs back and forth, very slowly. And then I saw dark shoes, big ones, coming close, and her legs got very still. It was my father," she said, and her voice, remembering, took on a sharp edge. "Can you believe that he picked my mother up and carried her screaming into their stateroom. I don't remember why no one tried to stop him. Maybe they did. He probably paid them off. He thought he could buy anybody with his wallet," she said contemptuously. "Anyway, he locked that poor woman in the cabin for twenty-four hours as punishment. Like an errant child. I still have trouble believing it," she finished, shaking her head.

Tama has lived with the man who fathered her child for four years. But she will never marry him. She is unequivocally opposed to the "false security of that legal tie." She insists their affair be always open-ended, including a still only theoretical possibility of sexual relationships with other people. As a matter of fact, staying unmarried has its share of complications. When they purchased a house, they lied about their status, and their tax returns don't allow them the same benefits they'd be entitled to as a married couple.

Jerry, her lover, is in fact becoming annoyed with the arrangement. Jerry's name appears on their daughter's birth certificate, but he worries about what they will tell people like school registrars. For that matter, he questions what they will tell the child herself. "I agree with Tama in principle," he says. "Marriage is an anachronism today. But we do love each other, and we are living together, so why not marry and save all this hassling?"

It's doubtful that Tama will change her mind, even if her stubbornness causes Jerry to leave (and there are some indications this might happen).

A marriage counselor told me that such fierce determination to "stay free of the history of being a woman," underlies many of the alternative family arrangements we see being made today. Tama is not a revolutionary. She is simply trying to break free of past systems of man-woman relationships that she feels were destructive.

"And, too," the counselor said with a smile, "don't make light of the idea that it adds a little bit of excitement to a relationship to know it's experimental. Also, it reinforces people's consciousness of their life together to know that *staying* together is a conscious act. Many young people are deeply resentful of the automatic pilot aspect of their parents' marriages. You know," he explained, "where you walked out of the church and didn't look where you were going till one of the partners died. Without the legal bond, you're there because you want to be there. That's important."

The "automatic pilot" aspects of marriage and family led many single parents to come into their role in a sense reluctantly. Marion had been having an affair with a married man for three years. She very much wanted to have a child. "All my life, I knew I wanted to have children," she says, "and the idea that I was almost out of my twenties and didn't have even one yet was absolutely astounding to me. I couldn't figure out how I'd gone so far off the track."

She asked Phil, her lover, many times to allow her to have his child, but he was adamantly against it. Finally, she made up her mind to try and become pregnant without his knowledge.

"I felt unhappy about doing it. But I wanted a baby, and there was no one else in my life. Besides, I wanted to have a baby by someone I loved."

However, Marion freely admits that underneath her very real desire to be a mother, she was hoping that becoming a mother would encourage Phil to make her his wife. In the world of her fantasies, she remained convinced that, despite Phil's anger at the news of her pregnancy, after the baby arrived he would get a divorce. Phil continually beseeched her the first weeks of her pregnancy to have an abortion. Although they weren't legal at the time, he found the names of high-priced practitioners and kept assuring Marion they would solve the problem in total safety.

Of course, Marion didn't see her pregnancy as a problem. She wanted a child, with or without Phil's approval, she told him, half-believing it herself.

"But still, there was that neurotically logic-tight place in me that went on spinning fairy tales for our future. I would have a harangue with Phil, and he'd walk out in a huff, and I'd go to bed all smiling and hopeful because the baby was kicking on the left side and someone told me that meant it would be a girl. I wanted a girl because Phil already had two sons, and I felt that a little girl would be even more of an inducement for him to leave his wife."

In the last two months of her pregnancy, Phil left for an extended business trip. With the inverted logic of irrational thinking, Marion, instead of being upset at his going, was pleased because he would be away from his wife. He returned a few days before her daughter's birth, "and the first thing he said to me when he walked through the door of my apartment was, 'I think you should see someone about giving the baby up for adoption.' I'd gotten one letter from him the whole time he was away, and it read like a goddamn travelogue, and that was his greeting to me. But then he got all loving, so much so that he almost convinced me maybe he was right."

The idea nagged at her those final hours of her pregnancy, but when she delivered a healthy daughter the fantasy of being Phil's wife covered it over.

"As soon as the doctor told me it was a girl, I was sure again that Phil would go right from the hospital to Reno. Incredible, what we can do to ourselves," she says wonderingly.

Phil, of course, had no intention of going anywhere but home to his wife. Marion insisted he look at the baby, but "he could barely have seen the color of her hair, he was back so fast," she remembers.

The moment he did come back into her room, he began cajoling her to give the baby up. He told her it would be better for the baby as well as herself. He was a lawyer, and Marion says she had the distinct feeling he had "prepared a brief" the same way he would try to convince a jury, with as much persuasiveness, and with as little real personal involvement.

But something upset Marion even more than his facile arguments about her welfare. "Although he didn't say it directly," she says, "I had the distinct feeling he was making a deal with me. If I gave the baby up, he would go on seeing me. Well," she said with a sigh, "fantasies die hard, but eventually they do die. He left the room and I knew I'd never see him again. It was a confrontation with reality that was long overdue."

In these last five years Marion has moved totally away from feeling that marriage is a necessary part of the good life. "I know now that it was being a mother I really wanted. I clung to Phil because I still had the feeling that I needed to be a wife before I could be a mother. Now I know the two rôles are separate. I'm not unequivocally against marriage, but I don't *need* to marry. And understanding that has a rather negative effect. It seems so unnecessary to me, that there would have to be a really overwhelming reason for me to want it. Besides," she finished, "the longer I go on living this way, the more reluctant I am to change. Someone else in my life, no matter how much I cared about him, could upset the whole balance of things."

As a psychologist said to me later, "nothing reinforces behavior more than actually doing something and doing it with some reward." Had Marion been unsuccessful as a single parent, she might have clung to the conditioned idea that she needed a husband to make being a mother meaningful. But her experience proved something quite the contrary.

"The fact is," this psychologist said, "that while everyone needs love, not everyone needs to be married. In a way that's always been true. Only women today are free to declare it and to act on it."

Women like Betty and Jean, both older adoptive mothers, also feel that the more time that goes by as single mothers, the less eager they are to change the shape of their life by bringing a man into it.

"Perhaps it's because I *am* older," Betty says. "But I really feel that what I want now is stability in a love relationship. I have that as a mother. Relationships with men are filled with wonderful emotional ups and downs, but that steady base of joy that I have with my daughter isn't there. I wouldn't want to tamper with that in any way."

And Jean, who is in her mid-forties, also finds being single very satisfactory.

"I suppose I've never been the kind of person who really wanted day-to-day intimacy with other adults. I adore being with children but I really tire rather quickly of other people, unless there's a true respect for the other's privacy. The one time I lived with a man, I found it very difficult that he would want companionship when I wanted to hole up by myself with a book—things like that. I was constantly feeling guilty and selfish, and finally, despite the fact that I really cared for him, I asked him to leave."

With her daughter, Jean seems able to satisfy her need for privacy more easily. "I just tell her I want to be alone for a while, and get her something to do. I don't know, maybe it's that she's always lived with my particular life-style, but we seem to move to each other's rhythms much more than I'm able to do with other adults. People of my generation generally have very different attitudes about 'closeness' from mine," she said musingly. "Too often for me, their idea is something very oppressive."

Actually, Betty and Jean's attitudes are quite unusual for women of their ages. It's generally a younger woman who declares marriage obsolete and moves into single parenthood without any suggestion of regret or apology. The conditioned idea that really they "should" be married nags at the consciousness of even the most liberated woman past thirty-five. Girls in their twenties, on the other hand, are certain and assertive about how little they need the certainty of legal marriage.

"When I discovered I was pregnant, Ben wanted to marry me immediately," says Sheila, a successful fashion designer in her mid-twenties. She had been having an affair with him for nearly two years. They maintained their own apartments but were with each other almost daily.

"But we didn't really love each other. Not in the way that would make us want to marry. We love a lot about each other, but marriage? No, there should be more."

So, despite Ben's very real desire to marry her, Sheila insisted on remaining single. Their child is now a year old, and Ben takes an active part in her life. But he agrees with Sheila that marriage would have been wrong. They have both begun to see other people and anticipate that the sexual side of their own relationship will soon end.

"If we were married and feeling this 'winding down,'" Sheila said, "I'd be panicking, or manipulating him to stay on with me. Or manipulating myself into believing I cared more than I really did. Divorce is ugly, no matter how civilized you are. It's much better that we loved each other and let the love fade in freedom. We will always care about each other and be there for each other. And our child has got to be better off than if we played games with our real feelings."

Critics of the single parent experience say that traditional motherhood was much more spontaneous and therefore, by their definition, healthier than Sheila's cool deliberateness. But, according to one psychiatric social worker, "I don't think that's much of an argument against single parenthood. Everyone has motives for everything they do. The trouble is that too often they're masked. There's a cause-and-effect sequence to life from the minute we give that first yell after someone grabs us and turns us upside down in the hospital delivery room. To open your eyes to the causes and effects of your experiences throughout life, I think is good."

For some girls, having a baby brought "cause" to lives they felt were empty of any. Although there is a suggestion of neurotic "need," here, professional people feel really good reciprocal relationships could still be managed. "As long as the girl realizes the child has his own needs, that the child fills many of hers, is not necessarily negative."

Nancy, the mother of a sixteen-month-old girl, illustrates this balance of needs. She had been, in her own words, "pretty freaked out" when she discovered she was pregnant. She'd been drifting on the edges of the drug culture, her own drug experiments rather superficial, but her detachment from the "straight" world quite total.

A senior-year dropout from a leading women's college, Nancy would work at odd jobs just long enough to pay the price of a plane ticket out of the country. With a backpack she'd drift from place to place, occasionally touching down to join that vague brotherhood of wanderers one finds in hostels throughout Europe.

The recipient at twenty-three years old of enormous freedoms—the options for a young woman have never been greater —Nancy found her life in chaos.

She discovered she was pregnant in Greece. Feeling rotten, she'd gone to an American doctor. His diagnosis rocked her, not only because it was so unexpected, but because it threw her sex life into a harshly vivid light.

"I couldn't even guess who the father was. I realized I'd had sex with a dozen different men that month," she says unsmilingly. "It really got to me that I'd been so"—she groped for a word—"so . . . random."

Not wanting to make any decision in Europe, she cabled her parents for money and came home. Her mother, already worried about where her daughter's life was heading, advised abortion. But for reasons she couldn't really articulate, Nancy preferred to have the baby, planning to give it up for adoption. About midpoint in her pregnancy, her father died of a heart attack and left Nancy a considerable amount of money. The shock of his death, the money now available to her, the long hours she spent while she waited for the baby in thinking about the last couple of years of her life, all began to influence Nancy away from adoption and toward the idea of being a single parent. The idea became decision when the baby was born. Her daughter so resembled Nancy's own baby pictures that, as she says, rather self-consciously, "giving her away felt to me like I'd be giving up on myself."

For the first year of the baby's life, Nancy did little more than stay home with her.

"I wanted to get my head together," she says. "I knew enough not to suffocate the kid. Don't forget," she says wryly, "I was a psychology major in college. I left her with baby-sitters even when I had no place to go. I'd just take off for the park or something by myself. I wasn't depressed or anything . . . just trying to find out where I was."

Had she found out, I asked? Yes, she said, she feels she has. Oddly, she's very involved in abortion reform, believing that for many girls her decision to have the baby would have been a poor one. Not all girls who drift through life lightly, as she was doing before Jennifer was born, could deal with the reality demands of motherhood.

Becoming involved in this reform movement helped Nancy grow more responsible. It represents to her becoming involved with life, "finding out what I believe, and acting on it—instead of letting everything act ON me." She said that her renewed sense of participation in her destiny would never have happened if she hadn't had the baby. Her commitment to her daughter and her ability to be responsible for her welfare put her life into a framework that she needed. Total open-endedness was more than she, and she feels most anyone, can handle.

"I like knowing," Nancy says with a smile, "that when I get that wanderlust feeling some nights, I *can't* just take off." Most psychological thinking supports the view that a sense of limits is important to people.

"It's like when you tell a child to draw something," a doctor explains. "You're generally better off giving some kind of guideline, 'Draw something blue, or funny,' than to just say, 'Draw anything you like.' Otherwise, the kid doesn't really know where to begin. Giving some sort of framework, no matter how broad, often results in a much broader sweep of creativity. In the same way," he continued, "most professionals agree that people really like to have boundaries for their behavior. Some sense of what the limits are. Otherwise, they can become terribly confused."

This man could understand how commitment to a child could impose such positive limits on a girl such as Nancy's life. But again the question arises, is this putting too much of a burden on that relationship? Does it imply that the child will be responsible for her mother's emotional health? This troublesome idea recurs when Betty says, "Adopting a child late in life made the difference between my life ending with a feeling of fulfillment instead of a sense of despair."

Many professional people, however, do not seem terribly distressed at such an open need to be a parent. The counselor who worked with Betty on her daughter's adoption was confident Betty would not use her motherhood in any way that would abuse her daughter's independent needs. "I'd guess," she said, "that more children are 'used' this way in conventional family situations than in single parent families."

Certainly, traditional parenthood is often a prison that traps both mother and child. Bored and restless women submerge themselves in futile attempts to make motherhood define their existence. They feel their own significance by "sacrificing" for their children. Too often, the interest a child has to pay back on these investments is exorbitant.

It seems reasonable to conclude after meeting many single mothers that unmarried motherhood can be rewarding to all kinds of people. Although they have arrived at the quality from different routes, they share a tenacious determination to steer their own lives. For a variety of reasons, some more positive than others, they have decided to leave the passenger seats to other, less adventuresome people.

Homosexual Parents

IN RESPONSE TO THE QUESTION whether a homosexual could raise a heterosexual child, a young lesbian answered with a smile, "But what kinds of homes do homosexuals come from now?"

It is this kind of answer that throws a swift jab to muscles primly tightened by tradition. The breath catches as rigidly frozen positions suddenly threaten to sag.

Now, wait. This is America. Land of the red, white, and blue heterosexual. New Jersey is not ancient Greece, you know. And how many beautiful young gladiators are really frolicking in the hills of Rome or Troy, New York?

Quite a few, it would seem. Only they are dressed in button-down shirts or overalls, and they work as teachers or laborers or doctors. Conservative estimates indicate that around 6 percent of adult males in this country are practicing homosexuals, while about 3 percent of women are lesbians. I call these estimates conservative, because homosexuals are just beginning to emerge from the "closet" where they have hidden their sexual predilections from any but their own guilty sight.

Much is written today about an apparent rise in homosexuality. Indeed, a great deal of the resistance to changing some of our laws against the homosexual is based on the fear that if society becomes more accepting, more people will choose the homosexual way of life. With apparently as much logic as our laws on prohibition had, the idea seems to be that by denying legal access desire will disappear.

At a consciousness-raising session of a lesbian mothers' group, Susan, the divorced mother of two sons, who now lives with her children and a lesbian lover, said, "I'm no more homosexual today than I was on the day I married my husband. I was just as much a lesbian when I had sex with my husband as when Hilary and I make love. I hid behind the heterosexual role all that time because I was afraid of what society would do to me if I admitted to being a lesbian. No, you wouldn't be raising the incidence of homosexuals if you eased the laws. All that would happen is that you'd finally get a chance to count how many there are."

Those who study social change seem to agree with Susan. There really is no evidence that the number of homosexuals has grown proportionately to the general population. But what has happened, it seems, is that awareness of homosexuality as an alternative life-style is starting to receive a higher degree of acceptance from the general public. Again, this has to do with the idea of plausibility. Behavior does not have to change for society to take new forms. All that has to happen is that certain "deviant" behavior begins to seem plausible, and therefore becomes more acceptable to society at large.

Refusal to yield to previously accepted criteria is at the heart of the issue of whether a homosexual can be a successful parent. The majority of homosexual parents either believe, or are trying very hard to believe after years of being told otherwise, that they cannot be judged as people by the style of their sex lives. Only if they continued to see themselves as deviant, with all the negative connotations of that judgment, would they judge *themselves* unfit to be parents. If they can truly believe, instead, that a person is much more than the sum of his physical parts or the sexual use of those parts, then they can relate to their children without guilt, as one human being to another. Well-adjusted homosexuals are those who feel that sex-differentiated roles are an anachronism today, and that their major responsibility to their children is a great deal more complex than whether they influence them to become heterosexuals or homosexuals.

Judy, an attractive lesbian who is the lover of a somewhat older woman, a successful pediatrician, came to the relationship after a two-year affair with a man. She says that she has always preferred women to men sexually, but that she is capable of loving a man, and of enjoying sex with a man she does love. She did, in fact, choose this man to be the father of her child. He stayed with her through the baby's birth, and then left for a job relocation in France. They occasionally correspond but he takes no financial responsibility for her daughter. At this point in Judy's life, she feels that her lover is her daughter's other parent, but she is unconcerned either that the relationship might not last through her daughter's childhood, although she feels it probably will, or that it is a relationship that is homosexual.

"I'm not ashamed that I love Laura [her lover], and I expect to have my daughter relate to her as I do, as a whole human being. What terrible thing am I exposing her to? She's going to grow up seeing two *people* who love each other and her very much. What difference does it make if one of those people has a penis or not?"

People are venturing into uncharted territory to find answers to these questions. It was much easier in many ways for society to function when it could be certain about what was normal and abnormal behavior. The recurring theme of this book is that the doors of all our closets have opened up, only to quickly close behind us as we hesitantly walk down virgin paths. And they lock away all the comfortable clothes of familiar roles and moral judgments. Dr. Philip Rieff has said that this climate of cultural revolution amounts to "permission for each man to live an experimental life," a good metaphor for the changing role of the homosexual in society.

The idea that the homosexual is a victim of uncontrollable impulses is at the root of much of his oppression. Going back again to the belief that his form of sexual expression is deviant (read *sick*), he becomes part of that nightmare-peopled country of our fears—the lurking rapist, the whip-carrying sadist, the leering Peeping Tom, and worst of all, the predatory child molester. All those terrible newspaper stories that we follow with morbid fascination—the child who was abducted on Monday, seen here on Tuesday in the company of a "masculine-looking woman" or an "oddly dressed man," and who by the weekend is found lying in some ditch, abandoned and broken—this filters through our consciousness when we realize someone is a homosexual.

Many men and women connect homosexuality with child molesting. A recent panel discussion about the homosexual as a parent found this question raised over and over again by members of the audience. Finally, one psychiatrist, who was quite traditional himself, answered a persistent woman in obvious exasperation, "My dear lady, don't *you* have any sexual impulses? Why should you assume that a homosexual with a child would have any less control over his impulses than you or your husband do over yours?"

Fay, a lesbian mother who also acknowledged her homosexuality only after several years of marriage, was involved in a bitterly acrimonious custody suit mainly over this point. She was eventually granted custody of her children, but not before she and the children suffered the kind of emotional pain that lingers even now, three years later. She is bitter about this concept that "what I do in bed determines what kind of mother I am and that my homosexual friends are going to do anything to my children that friends of my husband's wouldn't do."

Most homosexual parents have experienced at least one mother who wouldn't allow her child to visit in their homes; yet the fact is that homosexuals are no more likely to be sex criminals than heterosexuals are. One American Civil Liberties study, for example, showed that women, heterosexual and homosexual, were involved in 11 percent of felony arrests, but that only 2 percent of these were sexual offenses, and of these 2 percent, most had to do with prostitution and pandering. And the Sex Information and Education Council of the United States reported, "Sexual offenses by women against either male or female children are practically nonexistent," going on to say, "The man who is sexually interested in children is rarely a homosexual with well-developed interests in adult males, and he seldom is a member of the 'gay' community."

The original mocking question of the young lesbian about what kind of homes now create homosexuals clearly makes it difficult to defend the superior qualities of the heterosexual home. Actually, there is little agreement about whether it is an overbearing mother or a passive father, or a seductive father, or a man-hating mother that produces the lesbian or male homosexual. Few homosexuals are clear about what dynamic in their own homes may have contributed to their rejection of the heterosexual life. Many agree in part with a new medical theory that says there is a physiological component to homosexuality.

"It was just there, always with me," one girl said. Another young man said, "I never really consciously thought about it. Then one day I just walked into a gay bar and felt I had come home."

One rather sardonic homosexual summed up what I heard from several other people: "All I know is that a lot of my friends, like myself, got the message early in life that the heterosexual ride wasn't such a good trip. My old man and mother couldn't stand each other. Who the hell wanted to get in on that scene?"

Many lesbians in particular find in homosexual relationships great joy in physical demonstrations of affection and are usually also demonstrative with their children. They often speak of their own childhoods as being barren of spontaneous hugs and kisses, with just a general lack of warmth that they delight in now in all their love relationships.

One lesbian mother said, "I can't remember ever seeing my father kiss my mother. Ever. My son sees my lover and me showing affection all the time. He's got to have better feelings about people and love and loving relationships than I had."

These are, of course, idealized images of what a child raised in a homosexual home can feel. Reality problems still intrude, and children straddling the social codes of a marginal time are often confused. Lee, who also lives with her lover, said her nine-year-old daughter will push her arm away from the lover if Lee helps her out of the car, or in any way seems physically affectionate. "They won't understand," she told her mother once, pointing over her shoulder to neighbors watering their lawn.

Lee does try, though, to have her daughter see other homosexual couples with children so she doesn't feel quite so alone in her life-style. These play arrangements have other advantages as well. Many repressed questions come out in this environment that reveal all the children's concerns and confusions. Even the sheer mechanics of the situation can be puzzling to a child. One five-year-old boy who had only known a particular couple *as* a couple asked how they had gotten their children if they were both women. They explained that they had previously been married, and each had children from those marriages. This seemed to satisfy him, but as the woman said later, the important thing, *she* felt, was developing an awareness in the children that there are a variety of living arrangements, a variety of family relationships.

"Hopefully," one of the women said, "they can just develop the consciousness that some homes have a mommy and a daddy in them, and some have two mommies in them. I know it's not that simple," she said with a smile, "but we feel we're helping them to at least open up to more acceptance of themselves, and to their life, by seeing that they aren't so unique."

Such attempts to counterbalance traditional family structures seem worthwhile, because a surprising number of homosexuals, with the strengths of their new attitudes and organizational support, are living as homosexuals in conventional communities. While they usually do not flaunt their relationships, neither will they hide them if someone should ask. Like Lee, they are aware that they are exposing their children to potential conflict as the discrepancies between their lives and that of the community's becomes apparent.

All the mothers are concerned about whether they are imposing too heavy a price on their children for the way they as adults have chosen to live. But, like Lee, they feel honest handling will help the child cope with the conflict, and that this confrontation with reality is preferable to ghettoizing their way of life. "Sure, there are stresses," a mother says, "but I had stresses from my parents that I could never talk to them about. I'm perfectly willing to help my children find ways of dealing with the stresses they feel, and even to accept their anger toward me if it's a part of it. What I won't do is make them ashamed and guilty because we choose to live a particular way. Look," she said then, "in my neighborhood it's 'different' to have a peace sticker on your car, and we have that, too. Different is different, but it's not arbitrarily bad. I want my kids to know that, so they don't spend their lives trying to live up to someone else's image of what they should be."

One boy in his late teens, who lives with his mother and her lesbian lover now that his mother is divorced from his father, seemed to confirm this idea that lesbian motherhood should carry no apology. He said that the problems he was now in therapy for had nothing to do with his discovery at sixteen that his mother was having a lesbian love affair, a fact his father had revealed to him in retaliation against his wife. What really "crippled" him, Josh feels, is that his mother had spent the formative years of his life in unhappy self-denial.

"Our house was so bleak, so barren. There was always so much tension. Everyone was smiling and all this hate was underneath. Don't adults realize that kids always know when their parents aren't happy? All that schizophrenic denying makes you feel you're crazy yourself. 'Why do I think they're so sad when they're smiling like that and calling each other dear and stuff?'

"So I grew up thinking sex was bad because I never saw it in anything but a hostile atmosphere," he continued, "and I grew up thinking *I* was bad, because if I was good my parents would be happier—Christ! How much worse could it have been to live in the knowledge that my mother was a lesbian? She'd be different. But I felt so 'different' I could hardly function half the time."

And then he said something that is again a key to much of the feeling that the homosexual does indeed have the ability and the right, in this transitional age, to be a parent. "If my mother had been an authentic person, had lived her life the way she really wanted to live it, that's where *I* might have headed. Maybe I could have gotten rid of so many of the inadequacies I felt about not being strong enough, or sure enough as a male, and started thinking about what it meant to be a person."

Only a few years ago, standards for adoptive parents by the Child Welfare League included "the acceptance of sex roles" as one of the criteria. But that phrase seems quaintly archaic in the light of today's steady de-differentiation of the sexes. As a matter of fact, there is some sociological opinion that it may soon be easier to make homosexual adjustment than heterosexual. Dr. Alfred M. Mirande, associate professor of sociology at the University of North Dakota says, "It is the heterosexual, not the homosexual who has difficulty establishing his sexual identity in a society where sharp and easily recognizable differences between men and women are not drawn."

Even if this seems an overstatement of how far we have come from yesterday's concepts, there does seem evidence that today's world is at least a little more receptive to there being alternate concepts. The culture as a whole is less tight-lipped about its "deviants." Perhaps they do not yet send out Welcome Wagons, but they do allow them to live around the edges of the traditional good life. And there is even occasional acknowledgment that "they" in their way are living responsibly and productively.

The effect of this changing perception is vividly seen when we compare the ways in which younger and older homosexuals view themselves. The homosexual mother near forty is far guiltier about her children's sexual identification than the mother in her twenties. Irma, who has children in their early teens and who raised them alone since infancy after a brief and abortive attempt at marriage, says she was absolutely "paranoid" about making them homosexuals. Although she had lovers, she would never allow anyone to even spend the night in her guest room, let alone have them move in with her.

"Once my son wanted to bake a cake. I walked into the kitchen and saw him with an apron on and getting out the bowls, and I actually went over to him and knocked the bowl from his hand and slapped his face! Of course, it's the worst thing any parent could do in a situation like that, but I had simply panicked. The sight of him with an apron was like throwing acid in my face. I responded on instinct, on the instinct for survival—his more than mine." And then she told of how when her daughter asked for a racing car one Christmas, Irma went to a toy store and bought the most expensive doll in the place: $45 worth of frills and plastic femininity to overwhelm whatever leanings she had away from that identification.

"You have to understand," Irma says. "You have to know what pain I suffered in society for being a homosexual. As a mother, I lived in constant fear that I was going to be responsible for my children knowing that kind of suffering. It ripped me to pieces."

It was only through therapy that she was able to get through her "gut-deep" guilt over being a homosexual and being a homosexual parent. Her negative perceptions of herself began to lessen, and positive perceptions to take their place. The progress she made was intensified by membership in a homosexual organization.

The gay liberation movement has in fact done a great deal to ease the guilt of the homosexual, and nowhere is it more obvious than in talking to Irma's friend, Lucy, a lesbian mother who, still in her twenties, is some fifteen years younger than Irma.

"Irma told me that the first time she 'came out,' " Lucy says incredulously, "she went to one of those awful, gangster-controlled bars that I used to read about—you know, those places on dark streets in terrible neighborhoods where everyone looks like a bulldyke and they beat each other up and drink themselves unconscious."

Lucy finds this hard to believe because *her* first open experience with homosexuality was at a Daughters of Bilitus (the lesbian organization) dance at one of the most elegant hotels in New York City. No one got drunk, the clothes were worthy of any "ladies' magazine," and the atmosphere was gentle and gay in its realest sense.

Irma interjects to explain how the self-hatred of lesbians twenty years ago, hatred felt because of the culture's rejection and repression, made them hide out physically as well as emotionally in the darkest corners of life. Consequently, they were rarely able to relate to each other in any positive way because, as she says, "People who hate themselves can't love each other."

This incidentally is responsible for another prejudice against the homosexual as parent: that they are promiscuous, inconstant people, incapable of long-term relationships and commitments. Homosexual love relationships of recent years reflect the changing attitudes toward homosexuality. They belie the old self-fulfilling prophecy by frequently being life-time relationships that rarely could be judged as random and superficial. And all evidence shows that the thoughtful homosexual is as serious a parent as any heterosexual.

As the homosexual community accepts its right to full participation in society, its members turn more of their energies to the right to have and raise children. The doors through which a homosexual could bring a child into his or her life were not many in the past. Unless a woman married, she could not be a mother. Unless a man married, he could not be a father.

"The idea of single parenthood is the most liberating idea in the world for a lesbian," one mother told me. "If I had realized, even gotten the *thought* that it was possible for me to get pregnant without getting married, I would never have lived as Eric's wife for all those years."

Now some lesbians who do have the idea are deliberately becoming pregnant in some brief heterosexual relationship. Generally they do not tell the man who is responsible for the conception. But sometimes, as a woman named Arlene did, a lesbian and her lover will decide they want a child and will ask some male friend to help make this possible. Arlene had an old friend whom she had slept with once or twice before committing herself to homosexuality. After a year or so of living with her lover, Ellen, they asked this man, who had remained Arlene's friend, to cooperate with their wish to raise a child together. The child is now five years old, and the man remains close with the family, but in no way feels a need to make his contribution to the little girl's life known.

"Ellen and Arlene are her parents. It would be absurd for me to feel otherwise. I love Arlene and I'm happy I was able to contribute to her happiness. I don't feel degraded or used or anything but pleased with how it all turned out."

Some lesbians now are investigating the idea of using a sperm bank to conceive, again either raising the child as a single parent or with a lover who then becomes the child's other parent.

In this tale of another time, our time, adoption still remains a problem for the homosexual parent, which therefore makes parenthood a particular problem for the male homosexual. Actually, no law exists against a homosexual adopting a child. This is, of course, for the same reason that there were no laws governing air traffic before the invention of the airplane. As one adoption counselor told me, "We never even thought of the single parent adoption, much less that a homosexual would want to adopt a child. How could we make provisions for a concept we didn't have?"

Many homosexuals living as couples or alone are trying to

take advantage of this fuzzy climate to become adoptive parents. One homosexual couple, whose home meets all the state requirements for an adoptive home, except, of course, that two men occupy it instead of a man and a woman, are trying to make their case a test case. Privately the adoption agency has said it would welcome the case being tried, so that some precedent would be set. At the moment, it would be afraid of granting the adoption without this sort of support.

However in these days of legalized abortion, the adoption market is so limited that the homosexual parent will stand far back in line for being granted a child. We've come a long way, baby, but heterosexual couples are still considered the best parents for a baby to have. And as long as a single parent will only get the children married couples do not want, the single homosexual parent's chances for adoption are usually quite slim. Nonetheless, they are technically eligible to adopt as single parents and adoption agencies vary in their receptivity to the idea. A random sampling of several agencies showed the majority at least claimed a willingness to "consider each case individually." They all said they would certainly "encourage homosexuals to apply for adoption" in the same way that anyone else would receive encouragement.

The only open objection raised by the adoption agency was the need to ascertain that the prospective parent would not use his role as a parent to act out conflict or anger against society. But again, as an agency person said, "This kind of self-awareness is looked for in any adoption, and particularly in any single parent adoption, heterosexual as well as homosexual." However, while sex-differentiated identities may not be so important as we once thought, adoption personnel do worry about homosexual homes where the heterosexual sex roles were in fact replicated by the homosexual couple, being afraid this would cause a child serious confusion. Yet this too seems to be one of yesterday's concerns, as the majority of homosexual couples today do not act out the "butch" and "femme" stereotypes many of us still associate with homosexual relationships.

"Don't you see," Arlene patiently explained, "we were all

locked into the Doris Day, John Wayne bag—the homosexual as well as the straight community. We all had only two roles to choose from. So we chose like everybody else chose. You be giggly and feminine and I'll be powerful and tough. Why is it any different than the way straight women had to deny they were aggressive and independent because there was just no room for a 'woman' to be that way? Thank God we're all getting away from that. We can all stop role playing finally and just be people."

Over and over this theme is played. People. Wholeness. Its rhythm is insistent, particularly when it is heard in so many corners of our lives. Heterosexual marriages where contracts are signed dividing up the work without any sex-defined responsibilities. Or education that totally stops distinguishing between girls' courses and boys' courses. It becomes increasingly difficult to say because you are this sex, you are rigidly and irrevocably to stand in this role and should reject, usually in anger, anything that smacks of the other role.

Where *does* sexual identification come from in a transitional time of life? And what does sexual identification mean, and how important is it? These are questions still to be answered. Many therapists feel that a child can receive his identification from several sources—the media, school, the community. Barbara, a lesbian therapist, says that children of homosexuals may actually have an easier time forming a clear sexual identity because their parents will not reject whatever leanings they have, feeling comfortable with whatever the child seems comfortable with. Whereas many heterosexual parents, she believes, still impose their frightened determination on the child that he be exclusively heterosexual.

Whether children of declared homosexuals raised in homosexual households can be *exclusively* heterosexual is not known yet. I met several "secret" male and female homosexuals whose children were unaware of their homosexuality and had seemed themselves to make conventional heterosexual adjustments. I also met several children of homosexual parents who did know their parents' leanings, and who were generally bisexual themselves. But here again, we have to remember that bisexuality among young people from heterosexual as well as homosexual homes, is a quite common phenomenon today.

Obviously, many, many questions remain. Answers only grow out of experiential opportunities to see whether an idea really works, to see if the possibility is indeed possible. Meanwhile we should be open to the idea that what once seemed "impossible" might have been a mere problem of perception.

To say conclusively that the homosexual cannot raise children, because everyone knows the homosexual has "problems," does not in this age of new sensibility seem to be a particularly persuasive argument. As witness this response from a very, very straight psychoanalyst:

"If people with problems can't take care of children, we'd better all have our tubes tied and get vasectomies—because if that's the criteria, there's no one that will *ever* be able to take care of children."

Adoption

THE NEWS FROM MANY college campuses is that obviously pregnant students are likely to be approached by strangers asking if they want to give their babies up for adoption. Adoption workers throughout the country hear of lawyers paying high school students considerable sums of money to put them on to classmates who are pregnant. Nearly every adoption agency of any size has received calls from people offering as much as $10,000 to "knock the first name off the list." And hardly an obstetrician handles a stethescope who has not been offered similar bribes for the referral of an adoptable baby.

The implications of these events are obvious. The supply of adoptable babies is rapidly shrinking, and has thrown the whole adoption world into a state of crisis. The "underground" methods of adoption, the "gray" and "black" markets, attract more and more buyers. A gray adoption is a euphemism for a private arrangement that usually involves a lawyer who specializes in adoptions, and a cooperative obstetrician. The adoptive parents hire the lawyer who finds them a baby and finalizes the adoption in court some thirteen to fifteen months later. The black market baby is a child who has been adopted through direct contact with the natural mother. Generally her maternity expenses are paid by the waiting adoptive parents, and the adoption itself is handled through the courts. Meanwhile the establishment marketplace for adoption, the private agency, has much less to offer its potential customers. The depletion of "inventory" has caused adoption agencies to rethink their most traditional concepts, and some people feel adoption, as we knew it, will never be the same again.

The single parent figures quite prominently in the story of a shrinking baby supply. For not only does the shortage affect the person who would like to adopt a child as a single parent, obviously the single natural parent contributed to the shortage in the first place.

In 1967 the Child Welfare League of America, which sets the standards for its over four hundred member agencies, issued a statement announcing that several agencies were ready to consider single parent placements for the older interracial or even handicapped child who could not be placed in a two-parent home. In a symposium on social service around that time, the director of the Los Angeles County Department of Adoptions said that his department's philosophy "finally led us to accept that, not being able to find two parents for every one of our children, we had best find one-parent homes for some . . . to a child who may grow up without any family, the question of choice is irrelevant."

As conventionally childless families clung to the fantasy of golden-haired, blue-eyed, perfectly healthy newborn babies, the hopeful single parent accepted the reality of parenthood with an older, interracial, emotionally or physically handicapped child. Even then, however, the road to "making a house a home" was not always easy. One woman who adopted an interracial little girl three years ago said she was told by a social worker in the agency that the majority of board members disapproved of single parent adoptions. Therefore every time her name surfaced to the top of the list, she'd be shunted aside for another placement. These were babies of mixed races, but the situation had already begun to tighten up enough so that several couples decided they were willing to adopt the particular infant that might have gone to Betty, the prospective single parent.

"I became absolutely paranoid," she told me. "I kept calling the agency and tried to keep my accusations calm so they wouldn't think I was some sort of hysteric. But it was really getting to me badly. Then I was finally told there would be a baby available at the end of the summer that would most definitely go to me, and I was ecstatic." But about a week later she was invited to a dinner party and met a couple who taught at a nearby high school. They had two children of their own, but announced they had applied to adopt an interracial child. "My heart sank, just sank," Betty says. "I literally couldn't stay there with them, or I would have gone on my knees and begged them to wait until I had gotten my baby. I knew they'd get the child in mind for me, even though they already had a family. I went home and cried myself to sleep, and the next day I couldn't eat or go to work. The strain had just climaxed. I had waited too long, had had my hopes raised and lowered too many times. And then"—she turned and smiled as she lifted her daughter up on her lap—"and then I heard that this woman had discovered she was pregnant about two weeks later and had withdrawn her application. I'm an agnostic, but it almost made me believe in God again."

The agency counselor freely admitted that were Betty to apply today as a single parent, even though the board members are more sympathetic to the idea of single parents, she probably wouldn't have gotten her daughter. The distinction between adoptable and unadoptable children is not so sharp anymore. The current questioning of values has led many people to feel they can love children who are not mirror images of themselves.

As often happens, individuals move faster than the cultural institutions. Some adoption agencies therefore still cling to the old rules of matching color and religion between prospective parents and child. But if the traditional adoption agency is to stay in business, it almost has to relax its restrictions. And so, although it is often with some concern, agencies who would never have considered it before are now arranging transracial adoptions. One figure shows, for example, that 35 percent of Negro children placed for adoption in 1970 were placed with white couples, while the year before that, the figure was only 23 percent.

The single parent then, who has before this been the likely candidate for an interracial baby, will find some new limitations on available children. Most agencies, given comparable standards of health, stability, and other characteristics considered necessary in an adoptive home, would give a child to two parents rather than to one. However, even this may change. Many people in adoption are beginning to ask whether the two-parent family is in fact always the best family for successful child rearing. It is conceivable that soon, and perhaps in certain situations even now, a particular single parent will be matched with a particular child because they seem right for each other, even though a married couple would also have qualified and was interested in being that child's parents.

The reason there is basis for such hope is that thinking in adoption has dramatically changed. The push is really on to find homes for children who have never had any hope of having one. Yesterday's easy categories of "desirable home" do not work for today's realities, and adoption personnel are throwing over some old concepts with rather liberated abandon. The shortage of "premium" babies focused harsh light on the vast number of nonpremium children languishing away childhoods in a series of foster homes, or in impersonal institutions, where they are not even important enough to keep firm statistics on. Estimates of how many homeless children exist in our Norman Rockwell family-portrait society hover near a figure like 200,000.

In the new effort to find homes for society's cast-off children, the agencies are becoming more aggressive about getting their story across, taking newspaper ads or going on TV to reach the public. The New York Department of Special Services for Children runs a weekly newspaper ad showing a child available for adoption. A recent picture was of a mongoloid baby. Other babies with "defects" have already been successfully placed. In Los Angeles, a television program sponsored by the County Department of Adoptions has already placed several hundred "special needs" children. The thinking behind the newly dynamic approach is clearly to make the unadoptable adoptable, and traditions are stepped away from with no apology. As one adoption supervisor said, "Our goal is to find warm accepting homes for children who will otherwise never have one—it's time to stop worrying about whether the person is married, how much money he has, or what the color of his skin is."

Part of this process involves kicking over another hallowed concept of adoption. Adoption personnel have traditionally seen it as their function to judge whether a prospective home is suitable for an adopted child. Many people now feel that an adoption caseworker should instead concentrate on educating, rather than evaluating, a person who wants to adopt. Show them what is really involved in adoption, and then trust they will be able to make the decision of whether they should in fact become adoptive parents.

The idea of educating a client about adoption moves into the even more relevant question of what kind of child a person will adopt. Again, if the goal is to provide homes for children who need them, why cannot an agency help people become more flexible about their requirements? Many agencies are sending letters to their applicants for adoption, saying that unless there is such flexibility they might as well not apply. They invite the people to attend group meetings where some sensitive issues are raised. Increasing numbers of people, single and married, are attending these meetings, and, slowly, more and more "unacceptable" children are being seen with a new perspective.

A single parent who wants to investigate the idea of adopting a special-need child can, if adoption possibilities are limited in her community, inquire through the adoption agency about an organization called ARENA (Adoption Resource Exchange of North America). Established by the Child Welfare League a few years ago, it attempts to break the barrier of adoption that limits adoptive parents to children available in their state, and, of course, limits a child's chances for adoption as well. ARENA matches children and would-be parents on a nationwide scale.

Just as married black people are being encouraged by adoption agencies to adopt older black children through official channels, the black man or woman like Annette who wants to be a single adoptive parent will find much cooperation in adoption circles almost anywhere in the country.

On the other hand, the single white person who adopts a black child will find some controversy about his decision, just as a married couple would. In April 1972, the National Association of Black Social Workers condemned transracial adoptions at the group's major convention. Its members went on record as being "in vehement opposition to placing black children in white homes." Their feeling, shared by many black people not in social work, is that this practice robs a black child of his culture and threatens the preservation of the black family. This point of view usually also holds that a child will experience really complicated identity problems as he grows up. Other people, of both races, feel this is not necessarily the case, or at least does not have to be if the parent remains aware and sensitive to the child's needs.

The furor that resulted from the social workers' position largely centered on the idea that such a rigid attitude works against the best interest of many black children who, if not adopted by white parents, would not be adopted at all. Many black psychologists, psychiatrists, and adoption personnel angrily agreed that the ideal would of course be for a black child to find a black home but that most of all, he needed a home. And if a black one does not exist, it is a totally destructive attitude to say he should be left in a foster home or institution.

One single white parent who adopted a light-skinned interracial child feels it is possible to raise a strong and self-confident black child. She feels that the first few years of her son's life have been quite without problems, and she does not anticipate too many difficulties in the years ahead. They live in a town that concentrates on scientific research, and the high population of scientists and scholars provides an "accepting" environment. Certainly it seems to be true that there are places where such life-styles can flourish better than others. A single girl who lives in a factory town, where perhaps certain stereotypes still exist and resistance to change still prevails, might do well to reconsider her decision to adopt an interracial child. Even this mother, in her open community, admitted she had turned down a very black child at the time she adopted her son. She felt their differences would have been too "visible." While she herself felt no qualms about the combination of white mother and black child, the combined social experiments she was engaged in—single parent and interracial parent—seemed simpler performed in a lower key.

Most professionals agree, however, that a parent who legitimately feels able to cope with raising an interracial child probably will be able to cope with whatever negative feedback may result from her decision.

But opinion is pretty well shared that a person considering an interracial adoption should first of all have real knowledge of people of other races, and preferably friends among them. Romanticized pictures of "exotic" strangers are not the best route to building a close intimate relationship within your own home. And while it is not necessary to overstress the child's cultural heritage, there should be real respect for his identity as a black person, and for himself as an individual.

The other side of this coin is that a parent should not be motivated by the heroic thought that he or she is making up for centuries of oppression. The child should be wanted and loved for himself, and not out of the parent's desire to expiate social evils. It is too easy to make an adoptive black child a symbol of one's own liberalness, apology, or personal heroism. None of this is fair to the child, even if it may feed the unconscious ego needs of the single parent.

The single parent considering an interracial adoption should also try hard not to oversimplify the problems that will in fact exist for the child after adoption. Even in the most liberal community there are bound to be some unpleasant moments, and a child will need real help in fending off the sharp barbs of prejudice. White parents of black children must be ready for their children's negative experiences so they can help them cope without too much bitterness or turmoil. As I indicated before, studies show that parents who are most successful at interracial adoptions are people who are not terribly affected by other people's opinions. Instilling these values in their children is probably the best way to help them through the uglier parts of group interaction. Hostility and contempt from other people require great strength if one is to cope with them. There is no greater strength than strong feelings of self.

None of the single parents of interracial children I spoke to seemed unaware that they had taken on a particularly complex kind of parenting. But all seemed confident, and indeed were showing, that they could handle it. In different ways, they felt it implied an extra responsibility. Betty, for example, feels a particular need to have Kathi always looking impeccable. The child's closet is lined with an incredible array of clothes, like some storybook closet filled by a fairy godmother's wand. "I don't want anyone to have any ammunition for criticism. I'm going to so dazzle them with her physical perfection that they'd sound insanely influenced by prejudice if they criticized her on that level. Maybe I'm spoiling her, but I feel the more beautiful she is as an interracial child, the more she's got going for her. I want her to take real pride in herself. Not just the clothes, but grooming, manners, the whole bit. I want her to walk out into that world thinking she looks great—and then if someone doesn't like the color of her skin, it won't seem so important."

It is hard to know whether so much focus on the child's appearance is productive. Undoubtedly Betty will counter it with equal attention to Kathi's intellectual development, as Betty herself is a highly intelligent and successful woman. I could not help wondering whether Betty's eagerness to have her daughter be really "beautiful" stemmed from a lifetime of inferiority about her own looks. She was, in fact, a lovely looking woman in middle age. But it was easy to turn back the years and see her as a too plump adolescent and a too buxomly, short young woman. Her own mother had been glamorous, and undoubtedly had made her feel unable to ever compete on that level.

But even if she is in effect compensating, making up for her own empty spaces and ancient hurts, she is obviously primarily concerned about her daughter's welfare and recognizes that she does in fact have a child with special needs.

Other single parents may consider the adoption of a physically handicapped baby, or of an older child who may have an emotional handicap from having gone too long without love. Annette's daughter was twenty-two months old when she was adopted. Although the child was physically well, Annette knew she would have many emotional problems. Adoption people all tell stories of tiny infants who showed obvious adjustment problems even when adopted soon after birth. Sometimes only two or three weeks have been spent in the agency nursery or temporary foster home, but the move from one caretaking person to another, no matter how loving each may be, can cause real distress. Annette's professional insights allowed her to anticipate her daughter's difficulties in adjusting to a new life. For the most part she does not get too upset at what she sees, and goes to extra mothering lengths to help the child move out of her dismal past and into a happy future.

"She's quite depressed, mostly," Annette says. "Lethargic, down. I guess she's not a very pleasant baby to have around. But I see real changes lately, and I anticipate I'll see more as time passes. If I feel she needs outside help later on, of course I'll get it for her. Look," she finished, "as a single parent, I couldn't get a newborn infant, and I'd be a fool if I thought a child can spend her infancy unattended in a crib in some ward and hop into my life all smiling and ready for mommy!"

The idea of getting supplementary professional help is rather fundamental to the issue of adopting a handicapped child. Very often, many of the child's disabilities are correctable and only the fact that they are homeless keep these corrections from being made. One single man who adopted a partially deaf child arranged for two ear operations on a very limited income. His insurance paid most of the cost, and the surgeon was so impressed with their story that he drastically reduced his normal fee. The child now has two-thirds of his hearing restored and was able to transfer from a special school for the deaf to his neighborhood school, where with a hearing aid he is beginning to live more and more as a "normal" child.

Joe, the father, feels that being a father has taken on special meaning through his ability to give his son back his hearing. His delight in the child's own delight at suddenly being able to enjoy experiences always closed to him is quite exciting to see. If parenthood at its best should present challenge, and should be a place for mutually rewarding meetings, certainly this father and his son have met that challenge, and inhabit that place.

Each successful single parent adoption of any category child paves the way for other adoptions to occur. As they do occur, certain general guidelines are being followed by most adoption agencies. The principal issue in a single parent adoption seems to be the motivation for adoption. Exhaustive interviews attempt to establish the parent's motive for wanting to adopt, and whether the motive is a healthy one. There is nothing negative about a woman feeling she would be less lonely if she adopts a child. But if the loneliness is so abject, and so dominates her view of life, there would be legitimate doubt about her capacity to create what adoption counselors feel is the most positive kind of parental relationship—the ability to nurture and grow with a child. Rigidly neurotic needs that must be satisfied allow no real growth. A person who needs love and constant proof of love will suffocate a child, and even when done in the name of love, this behavior will cut off a child's chances for a healthy life of his own.

This is why agencies will usually go deeply into the single applicant's interpersonal relationships as well as into her general history. How full is her life already? What relationships exist? How many really good friends of both sexes? How about love relationships with men, or, in the case of a male applicant, with women?

One adoptive mother told how she had gone out of her way to be "pure and virginal" in her interviews with the adoption agency, only to discover through someone who worked there that it was this very quality that was working against her.

"What they really wanted to know was whether I was a healthy heterosexual, capable of having satisfying relationships with men. Here I'd been desperately keeping it a secret that I'd been having an affair with a man for over a year, who I didn't really love but had very warm feelings about. When I realized where their heads were at, I told my counselor about it. Then we got into a lot of questioning about his visits, my attitude towards sexual display, and the like. But I knew she was much more sympathetic to my application after she had made sure of my sexual identification."

Jean was the first single adoptive parent in the state in which she lives. The idea of adopting a child had teased around various stages of consciousness for a long time. In an article about single parents elsewhere in the country, the supervisor of an adoption agency in Jean's community was interviewed. The woman said she would not be unsympathetic to the idea, though such adoptions would be granted on an individual basis, with each person being considered for himself and not as fitting into some existing policy.

On the strength of this, Jean called the agency and was quickly granted an interview. It turned out to be the first of many. She met the supervisor at least once a month, and frequently twice a month, for the next six-month period. She says with a laugh that "it was something like analysis."

In addition to their meetings, Jean filled out forms that asked such questions as what kind of physical arrangements could she live with, and what limitations would she find unacceptable in a child. Many of the questions she answered in writing, even though she also discussed them with her counselor.

For example, did she want a boy or a girl and why? Did she have feelings about an interracial child? Jean did eventually get a white child with a hip dislocation that was later corrected, but she had made it very clear she would feel comfortable with a child of any race. Although she preferred a girl, simply because she felt she had more to offer a girl in terms of sharing activities, she was totally open to taking a boy. There is no fixed feeling among agencies about whether it is better for a single parent to take the same sex or opposite sex child. Psychological opinion goes either way with arguments for healthy sexual adjustment made about both kinds of relationships. This matter will be discussed fully in the chapter concerning psychological development of the child.

As the meetings went on, Jean was probed more and more to determine, she felt, the stability of her personality. Her work habits, her entertainment habits, her general life-style were explored. She was asked about her basic philosophy toward life, and toward a child's needs.

At the time this process was taking place, Jean happened to be taking two courses in early childhood education. When she told her counselor about some of the papers she had written, she was asked to bring them into the agency so they could be read. It is interesting that Jean never resented this really intense kind of interrogation. Nor did Betty, when she told me much the same story of the preliminaries involved with her own acceptance as a single parent. Thoughtful people themselves, they appreciated the efforts being made to make the adoption as legitimate a decision as possible.

One of the things Jean had going for her was an unusually fine plan for potential child care. If a single parent has to work, as most do, the agency will insist on assurances that there is stable, available, and consistent care for the child. In addition, most agencies will look for some kind of extended family possibility. They will want some evidence that relatives or close friends exist, particularly of the opposite sex, who will allow the child intimate contact and identification with parent surrogates. Such relationships promise help to the child should the single parent be sick or for some other reason temporarily unable to care for him. The richer these resources are, the clearer the availability of people willing to participate in the child's life, the better chance a single parent has for being granted adoption.

Jean's arrangement satisfied both the day-to-day child care requirements and, even more importantly, the extended family concept. As a young girl, Jean had come to this country with a friend. They were graduate exchange students, but both elected to stay on in the United States when their educations were completed. They continued to be unusually close, representing to each other the family they had left behind in Europe. Even when her friend married, the relationship continued. In fact, it deepened, as there was exceptional rapport between Mary's husband and Jean. He appreciated Jean's interest and help to his wife, particularly when he had to serve in the army and she was pregnant with their first child. They always lived in close proximity to each other, and shared in each others' lives.

Early in Jean's decision to adopt a child, she told her friends about it and continued to keep them involved, as they wished to be, with the procedure. One evening she told them that she had been asked about the child-care arrangements she would make if she had a child. It was Jean's feeling that the counselor had wanted to catch her off guard—"to throw out a sticky situation and see how I would handle it." Jean felt, in fact, that she had handled it well. She was absolutely clear and unapologetic about her plans.

"I told her I would do what every other working mother does," she said. "I shall have to rely on baby-sitters."

But when her friends heard this, they immediately said they felt as three adults that they "should be able to care for one child." David, the husband, called the agency and arranged to go there with his wife and discuss their role in Jean's decision to adopt a child. The agency went into the dynamics of this decision, making sure that the arrangement was positive and well thought out. And it certainly appears to be. No one seems unduly martyred or beholden. They all say, and seem to mean it, that it is a mutually satisfying arrangement. As parents of three sons, the couple enjoy having a little girl around, and feel their boys benefit from the competition and reflection of a "sister." As for Jean, she sticks closely to a set of procedures they all worked out together. She drops her daughter off every morning on her way to work, but on weekends, when her friends are more involved with independent needs, she always hires a baby-sitter if she wants to go out. The same is true after dinner time during the week. She never calls on David for physical help unless no outside help is available. There are other self-imposed restrictions as well, that seem to keep friction totally removed from the experience.

Betty had no such plan going for her, but she carefully made baby-care arrangements with a young student nurse before her second interview with the agency. And as soon as she heard she was officially eligible for adoption, she contracted with a mother's helper to come over from Ireland and live with her. Betty had worried about not having a close enough relationship with her family. Indeed, she suffered a really painful blow when her brother reneged on his promise to be her child's legal guardian after learning the child was interracial. However, the rest of Betty's professional and personal life was quite rich with people. The agency clearly felt that a child would have a variety of positive interpersonal relationships with Betty as its mother.

As I have already implied, the fuller a single parent's life, the greater are his or her chances for getting a child through a private adoption agency. In fact, the single parent has one advantage over the married couple in adoption in that being "older" is viewed as a positive, rather than negative, factor. Agencies have seen many young girls who kept natural children and then became embittered at having given up their youth for premature motherhood. In the single parent, therefore, they look for someone who has already satisfied the headier needs of youth and is ready to settle into, and enjoy, maturity. Such a person will generally not regret the restrictions caring for a child often makes on a life, or feel particularly deprived by them.

Both Jean and Betty bear this out. While they enjoy their careers as well as being successful at them, they treasure the time they spend with their daughters and are constantly looking for ways to arrange their schedules so more time is available. Again, because they want to, not because they feel they should want to, or have no other choice. They chose to be mothers, and they seem happily to be living out that choice. Agency personnel are sensitive to this. "Contented people make good parents," said one supervisor. "The quality of time a person spends with her child is much more important than how much time, unless of course she's really excessively absent. It does no one any good to give a child to a woman only if she gives up a job she really enjoys. It's unrealistic and usually unproductive."

One of the things adoption agencies do try to make clear to single parents is that such adoptions can involve some special kinds of problems later on. The old problem of when and what to tell an adopted child can be intensified in a one-parent family. In addition to the child wanting to know why he was given up for adoption, he may want to know why it was decided he should be placed in a one-parent home. Particularly if the child is raised in a fairly conventional community where most families have two parents, he may feel an element of discrimination in the fact that he was given to a single parent. These feelings are not always articulated nor, in fact, are they always conscious, but they are questions many professionals are anticipating as the single parent phenomenon increases. There may also be more impetus, and even pressure, for the single parent to tell the child that he *is* adopted. In a traditional family setting, the facts of the child's adoptive status can be hidden for quite a while, although few families practice this pretense for any length of time. Nonetheless, the single parent is much more likely to get more questions earlier than other adoptive families, because the difference in family makeup is so obvious.

Advice on this is still hard to come by, because there is little precedent yet established. So far agency people feel it will be their job to support the adoptive parents in these situations, and help them develop the kinds of responses that will satisfy a child's needs and negative feelings. Agencies see their counseling services continuing over a considerable length of time.

A minor problem for the single female mother is that some people may be suspicious that her child is not really adopted, suspecting instead that it is an illegitimate child of her own. Once again, evidence suggests that the woman independent enough to be a successful single parent remains generally independent of other people's opinions. However, agency people do feel in this instance, too, a responsibility for helping a parent who feels she needs help to cope with the situation.

The availability of counseling is only one of the reasons many people are troubled about a movement away from the private agency to the independent adoption. At any time during the probationary period of an adoption through a private agency, for example, a parent can change her mind about her decision, or merely about the particular child she is considering.

Sometimes a child proves to be physically defective or has some emotional problems that were not picked up earlier, or perhaps the parent was simply unable to handle the child, no matter how good her intentions. An established agency will be open to helping a parent deal with such problems and even, if necessary, will take the child back.

It is this ominous phrase, "take it back," that really haunts the atmosphere of gray and black market adoptions.

Although (and this is perhaps the exception that proves the rule) the famous Baby Lenore case was handled through a private agency, the gray and black market adoptions seem to leave much more room for a change of heart by the natural mother. It is thought that the Baby Lenore case, which represents an almost unique situation in private adoption circles, was precipitated by the quality of counseling the mother received while pregnant. In any case, many more such stories occur *outside* the province of established adoption channels. For one thing, the secrecy that is so much a part of private adoption is not generally part of the fabric of independent adoption. In these cases, the natural mother is usually aware of who adopted her child. Even if she is unlikely to change her mind, many adoptive parents recoil at the idea that she could always locate them and decide to reappear, even temporarily, in her child's life.

In actual fact, the concept of secrecy is another concept turning around at different speeds now than it has in our past thinking. A number of people will argue that an adopted child grows up with obsessive identity questions that would be answered if he were allowed to find out who his natural parents were. The Child Welfare League has always adhered to the view that background information about an adoptive child be sealed permanently, and this is the case in almost every private adoption. Birth records remain forever hidden, and can usually be opened again only under court order.

Whether or not it is best for a child's psychological development to know his total history remains unanswered. Revolutions continue in adoption procedure, with many people making test cases, and much being written pro and con.

It may seem tempting to a single parent to try for a white infant through independent adoption, but she should be extremely careful about the people she engages in these procedures with. In periods of high demand, abuses occur. Unscrupulous lawyers and doctors have always hovered on the edges of the adoption market. But as the demand for their "product" rises, they proliferate, and can cause a great deal of damage to a great many people.

By way of illustration, there are legal loopholes within every state that affect the adoptive parent. In Florida, for instance, even if a woman is separated from her husband and becomes pregnant by another man, she must still have her husband's consent to place the baby for adoption. An adoption lawyer that ignores this legal wrinkle promises an adoptive parent little peace of mind.

New legislation has been passed concerning the legal rights of the unmarried father. An independent adoption procedure that is based on old concepts of his status might end badly. The father of an illegitimate child could wish custody of the child the mother gave up for adoption, and today the outcome of such a custody suit is not so certain. Careful scrutiny of the laws, and the changes in those laws, is extremely advisable to anyone contemplating an independent adoption.

Many people object to the idea of independent adoption simply on the ground that it seems immoral and distasteful, the flavor of the marketplace too pervasive. The baby goes not to the best potential parent, but to the highest bidder. Even if these objections are excessive, advice seems unified for the single parent to move cautiously if she moves away from established methods of adoption. There are already so many special aspects to her situation, that giving up the support of established procedures and services may be regretted.

Whatever the decision on how to adopt, the major issue is to be aware of your own motives for wanting to adopt. Becoming a parent can be a really joyful experience, but there are real stresses involved. If the single parent adoption has evolved out of loosened interpretation of what a family should be, so the single parent should loosen her hold on fantasized images of what it can be.

As one unmarried mother told me, "I found the change in responsibility overwhelming at first, but I discovered life without that responsibility wasn't really worthwhile." Most adoptive parents agree.

Natural Motherhood

AN UNMARRIED MOTHER who gave her baby up for adoption four years ago bitterly attacked the counseling she had received from an adoption agency.

"Now they're *giving* adoptions to single parents, and with me, they were so sure, so goddamn positive, that a child had to have two parents. Going to them for advice was like going to Spiro Agnew for advice on how to stay out of the army!"

Her bitterness is understandable, but sadly, so is her story itself. No counselor at any time would be justified in coercing a mother to give up her baby, but until recently, traditional thinking in adoption circles has been to advise the mother that such a move is desirable.

Social service personnel have always known that advising a mother whether or not to keep her child is an enormous responsibility. But like all other responsibilities, it is less awesome if the guidelines are sharply drawn. And so, again, in those yesterdays when lines were sharp and stood firm between right and wrong, agency counselors knew with certainty that it was indeed better for a child to be raised by two parents. Just as they *knew* girls who became pregnant "out of wedlock" were generally unstable. Just as they *knew* society would not accept the unmarried mother into its perimeters. And they *had* to advise adoption because they also knew that abortions were illegal, expensive, and dangerous.

These were the "hard facts," those beloved tools of the social scientist from which conclusions are drawn and judgments about behavior made. But suddenly, the hard facts are going flabby and soft in the center of today's experience. For times change, and as they do, perspective must also change so that the facts are seen from a more relevant point of view. Sometimes that perspective takes such a wrenching shift that the facts disappear entirely, leaving great empty spaces that must be filled all over again.

The traditional philosophy of the social service profession has made some of its personnel reluctant to keep step with the more recent changes in today's society. Their old ethics prevail, no matter how much prodding from their more flexible peers about the need to keep up with the times. It is difficult to find any professional writing about adoption or pregnancy counseling that does not contain some statement aimed at shaking up the dust of old ideas. Throw out the stereotype of the unwed mother, these articles say. It is a concept too filled with mythology and prejudice to base any programs on that will be meaningful today. Yet, like Diogenes with his lamp, looking for an honest man, some social workers still peer out in the fading light of their inherited beliefs, looking for the sad, depressed, unstable single pregnant girl. And seeing her in this light, they of course hold tight to the other traditional concept, that her child will be better off in an adopted home.

"The best interests of the child are rarely served by staying with the unmarried mother," one adoption supervisor told me, echoing many of her colleagues across the country. This phrase, "best interests of the child," is a tough one to deal with, for who of course could want anything else? But, as the late

Alfred Kinsey observed, there is a tendency in people to string together ideas in a supposedly casual sequence that in reality are based on a particular personal bias. Therefore, the conclusion that a child was better off with two adopted parents than he was with one unmarried parent, was greatly influenced by the bias of society toward the unmarried mother. Obviously, if the unwed mother is going to be discriminated against in society, her child will suffer more than the child of a nuclear family will. But if the mother moves into the cultural mainstream refusing to accept the second-class status of her "stigma," why should her child's best interests not be served as well, and perhaps better, by her? "And what about *my* best interests?" Jo Ann, a mother who kept her baby, shouted when we discussed the issue of pregnancy counseling. "You'd think the mother was absolutely irrelevant. Doesn't counseling have to include someone besides the child?"

It should, of course, and generally today it does. Social service agencies serve a multitude of purposes, not the least of which is to help a pregnant girl make the decision she really wants to make about her child. We are not "baby snatchers," agencies say firmly, hoping to dispel any timidity toward using their services. Most single mothers do feel the need for some kind of counseling when they discover they are pregnant. Even girls who had deliberately conceived looked for advice about the pregnancy, or arranging the birth, and later about being a parent. Friends and family, no matter how loving, are often not objective enough, or so the girl feels, to answer particular kinds of questions. Generally this judgment is true, but it is often especially true for the girl who is ambivalent about her pregnancy. And here, the need for really good professional counseling is crucial. The infamous Baby Lenore case revolved around the question of whether the natural mother had really received the proper kind of counseling. Had she in fact, however subtly, been influenced to give her baby up for adoption before really coming to this decision herself?

Considering the economics of the adoption market, or just the frailties of human nature, it is conceivable that such influences occasionally exist. Certainly Jo Ann will say they do. As far as she is concerned, all she ever was to the agency she visited was the source of another baby for one of their clients. "They had their hands on it the minute I first walked into that office. In retrospect, I feel like I was Hansel in the cage when the witch was fattening him up for the kill. I pushed my big belly through the door for my appointment every month, and that bitch of a caseworker had all she could do to keep her hands off me to see how close she was getting to what was inside!"

Jo Ann was unsure of her feelings when she sought pregnancy counseling. Although she had thought many times about becoming pregnant during a three-year love affair with Peter (now a potential father without knowing it), he was against the idea. He "wasn't ready" for marriage; but if Jo Ann became pregnant, he said, he would feel obligated to marry her. This somewhat outdated ethic made Jo Ann respond with an ethic of her own. She would not become pregnant without his consent because that would be "pressuring" him into marriage.

Only when it was apparent that the relationship was breaking down did Jo Ann begin to think of becoming pregnant again. She was twenty-eight years old and felt she should have a first child before much more time passed. Very deliberately then, she conceived, and as soon as she did, she encouraged Peter to end their affair by moving out of the apartment they shared into one of his own. "But the night he left," she recalls, "I went into a terrible depression. I'd been so proud of myself, wheeling and dealing and manipulating everything so I could become a mother. But all of a sudden when I was really alone in the apartment for the first time in three years, and really alone with the fact that I was pregnant, I absolutely panicked. I needed help very badly."

Because she felt so suddenly incapable of making decisions, she first told her parents the news, and then sought out the services of a private adoption agency. It took a few weeks to arrange an appointment, and in the interim her parents continuously pressured her to arrange for the baby's adoption. She was not feeling particularly well, and her social life was quite barren because she had been out of touch with any men but Peter for such a long time. Just about everything that in fantasy had seemed so easy now looked grim and frighteningly difficult. When the day of the appointment finally arrived, ushered in by a breakfast phone call from her mother repeating her monotonous message, Jo Ann was nearly paralyzed with ambivalence. It was not a surprise to her, then, to hear herself say to the counselor in an air of surrender that she planned to give her baby up for adoption.

"But anyone with one semester in psychology could see how fragile that decision was," she says contemptuously. "I resent terribly that they never really explored the alternatives to what I felt then was something I had to do."

Theoretically, a social service agency, public or private, should provide the widest gamut of services, so that there *is* the widest opportunity for a free choice of alternative decisions. The alternatives themselves for how to deal with an "illegitimate" pregnancy have never been broader. Almost any decision is now acceptable within the culture. Abortion is sanctioned, the pregnancy itself is at least tolerated by most of society, and a kind of counter-cultural courage prevails that makes many girls feel totally capable and unapologetic about raising children outside of marriage.

On the other hand, it is a psychological truth that freedom of choice often produces its own kind of anxiety. And so, because this is a book that in part speaks to people who are still only considering being single parents, it seems important to discuss what the alternatives are to that decision.

When a pregnant girl goes for counseling, she should try to determine how objective the counselor really is. Is the advice, in fact, colored by the counselor's professional needs or emotional bias? No one is immune to professional competitiveness. Occasionally abortion counselors will accuse adoption personnel of pushing for adoption while people in adoption will say, of course, the reverse.

Abortion counseling has increased because abortion today is

a legitimate and generally safe alternative to pregnancy. But even in this contemporary climate, there are factors involved in making the decision that should be balanced against its availability. The major consideration is actually the same one, though in a slightly different perspective, that applies to the single girl who decides to keep her baby. Or to follow out the line of choices, who decides to give her baby up for adoption. Be sure the decision is thought out and really is an expression of emotional and reality needs.

Those who ascribe to the theory that most unwanted pregnancies have a deliberate unconscious dynamic worry about the merchandising of abortion as an easy way out of unplanned motherhood. The personal and interpersonal psychological makeup of the girl, and of her relationship with the baby's father, is believed to be an important issue in whether or not she should have an abortion.

It does seem true that the decision to leave out a diaphragm, or skip a pill, or to, in other words, "take a chance" is generally less whimsical a decision than it appears to be. Many times, the girl is simply allowing herself to get closer to her real desires by letting up the controls of her conscious mind. In such cases, pregnancy is neither unwelcome nor unable to be dealt with. In fact, most of the time the event is met with great joy that "the decision was taken out of my hands!"

But, as I discussed in an earlier chapter, many "unplanned" pregnancies stem from unresolved emotional problems: a need for love, competition with a mother, a masochistic need for punishment—any ingredient in that mélange of distortions that mold our behavior. In these cases, abortion of the pregnancy may also abort the chance to resolve that problem in any permanent way. It will lie there still, long after the operation is over, always ready to demand again that it be heard.

Every adoption agency knows girls who call up saying they had an abortion three months ago and now are pregnant again. One supervisor told about a girl she had just finished speaking to. "She wanted to know, *now* what should she do," the woman said with a sigh. "What I tried to have her see, was that even if it were medically advisable for her to have another abortion so quickly, psychologically it would be the worst thing for her to do. The first abortion had solved nothing, answered nothing. But maybe," she mused, "if she goes through this pregnancy, has the baby, and either gives it up or decides to keep it, she might release herself from the controlling force of that need."

When I asked whether a girl so obviously confused could in fact be successful as a single parent, the answer was yes. "If," the supervisor explained, "she is a healthy enough person to understand what had really happened to her and why it had happened, and what her problems are in terms of relationships, then yes, she could keep her baby in a meaningful way." Again, the multipurpose agency will provide counseling for girls such as this one all through a pregnancy, aiming at helping them gain as much insight as possible, so that their choices of action are freed from the pulling restrictions of unconscious drives.

The other side of this coin, however, is that more and more people do have abortions with apparently little guilt or lingering regret. The old idea that girls who had abortions were potentially open for serious emotional problems is today widely disputed. One study, for example, showed that 75 percent of a group of women who had had abortions reported improved emotional health, a judgment that was confirmed by psychiatric evaluation. A total of 23 percent believed that the abortion eventually led to their emotional growth, and only 2 percent of the women in the study regretted their decisions to abort the pregnancy.

Still the guilt may persist, and many girls are psychologically afraid of abortion. It may be done now in a hospital, with perhaps your own gynecologist at the table, but the folklore of our childhood paints the picture over with one of seedy back rooms and dirty drunken butchers masquerading as doctors. Or we are religiously influenced in spite of our ostensible amusement at old-fashioned ideas such as sin and retribution. "I thought of abortion several times, but when you've been conditioned by religion since you were a baby yourself, believe me it's impossible," one girl said. Others who thought of abortion, and at one time almost every pregnant girl did, say vaguely, "It just didn't seem right. . . ." or "I just couldn't. . . ." When pressed, they remain vague still, and it is not hard to see the threads to the past behind their attempts to explain. Many girls played back and forth with the idea of abortion for months. Like Ilse, now a happy mother of a two-year-old daughter, it seemed the easiest solution, yet something kept her from going ahead and making it her solution.

"I had actually finally talked myself into it," she said, "when I felt life. And that was it. Abortion was from then on out of the question. It's one thing to terminate something abstract, but when you're made really conscious that there's a human life inside you, well, I'm not religious but that's another matter entirely."

A lot of single mothers report similar experiences. "Once you feel that baby move, forget it. He's yours," is said in some way over and over again.

This instinctual reluctance to tamper with life was at the heart of many decisions to discard abortion as a possible alternative, even when the pregnancy was really unwelcome. Several girls, however, again in retrospect, accuse the counseling they received. They feel it did not allow them to get rid of superstitious guilt so that they could, in fact, consider having an abortion. Particularly counseling that was religiously based they felt was also religiously biased, even when theoretically there was no secular law against legal abortion.

"That old 'sanctity of life' syndrome," Elizabeth says wryly. "But no one ever talked to me about the sanctity—or the *sanity*—of what *my* life was going to be like as a single mother!" Elizabeth became pregnant at a point of great change in her life. She had broken up with her fiancé to pursue an art career, leaving her southern hometown for Boston and art school. Her parents were furious and swore they'd never "bail her out" if she got in trouble. Although she had been sleeping with her fiancé for over a year, with very careless attempts at contraception, she had never become pregnant. But two weeks after meeting someone in Boston, one month after starting school, she was a prospective mother. There was no one to talk to. She had not been in Boston long enough to make any real friends. The man involved was involved with her in only the most casual way. Through the yellow pages she found a counseling service that was part of the church affiliation of her childhood. It was not Catholic, but, Elizabeth says, "it might as well have been."

The idea of abortion was certainly unpalatable to her at the time, but she feels now had someone really explored the question with her and explored the future effects of her decision to keep the baby, she would have been open to changing her mind. Because, she says now, "If I could turn back the clock, I'd be on the table with my legs spread apart in five seconds flat. I should never have had my baby."

If her honesty is startling, we have to remember that it *is* honest. Single women who have children when they are on the threshold of new life experiences may find the experience of motherhood joyless and often deeply despairing. For while single parenthood is in many ways an expression of freedom, the life of a single parent can sometimes severely lack any opportunity for freedom.

Elizabeth's eyes flash in hungry fantasy when she speaks of what life "might have been" without the insistent demands of a child to fulfill. Her daughter is two now, an age Elizabeth finds particularly intolerable as she tries desperately to pursue her painting.

"I have to lock up my paints if I want to go to the bathroom, for God's sake, so she won't get into them. Or I have to break away just when I'm really getting into something because she fell, or she's wet, or wants something to eat. And I have to work at these dumb part-time jobs that sap me creatively. And then I come home and instead of having a drink and falling into bed, I've got to make the goddamn lamb chop and vegetable and read to her and bathe her. By the time she's asleep I'm too wiped out to work and too overtired to sleep.

I'm so incredibly restricted. I've given up so much freedom, in every way. Physically and emotionally and intellectually. Just when I was at the point of becoming my own person, I inflicted myself with a totally dependent person who makes me always respond to *her* needs. I hate it. You can't imagine how I hate it," she says, seeming to defy the listener to pass judgment on her as a cold and unloving human being. It is a judgment I did not make, because her own pain and conflict are so apparent.

"Listen," she says then, "you tell people not to do this unless they've really got a lot of money, or are really established in what they want to do. The guilt you feel all the time about your own feelings, the anger . . . God, the anger is so great it terrifies me sometimes. I don't know what's going to become of both of us, whether we'll ever really have a relationship that's worth anything. I try not to show her how much I resent her, I try to have only the love show." She looks up and adds, "I do love her, you know. . . . But I hate her more."

The fact that many girls feel this kind of whirling confusion, either when they first realize they are pregnant or when they face the realities of being a single parent, led one girl in Chicago to form an organization called Mothers Alone. It is incorporated as a nonprofit association for unmarried mothers in the Chicago area. As word of its existence grows, it is highly possible that other mothers in other parts of the country will either affiliate with it or create similar groups of their own. The desire to talk to other people who have shared the experience of unmarried pregnancy is often great. There is a feeling that, together, people might give each other support and work out solutions to mutual problems. The girl who created Mothers Alone said, "I've been there and I know what it's like. You don't want sympathy, you want help. I think if I had had some contact with others in similar situations it would have helped me. I think every woman should have the right to determine what her feelings are and where she wants to go without pressures and threats."

Too often, where to go for the many decisions necessary in single parenthood is limited by the inadequacies of a particular counselor and his personal bias. In large city agencies, for example, many people stay in their own little bureaucratic niches, never really knowing what the total range of the agency's services are. Many people who went to public agencies complained they were not "given the whole story" and, worse, were often given misinformation. Ilse, for example, told a tale that sent an adoption lawyer hearing it into apoplectic fury. She had gone to the Department of Special Services in her city for counseling and was quickly advised by the counselor to give her baby up for adoption. He felt that a baby should have two parents. ("*A* baby, never *my* baby," Ilse points out, illustrating the frequent inability to see beyond a professional "approach" to the dynamics of an individual case.) The counselor, as a means of convincing her, assured Ilse that she could always get her baby back "if she changed her mind."

"I knew that was ridiculous," Ilse said, "and I asked him wasn't there a date beyond which the natural mother had no more legal rights. . . . He just waved that away as a formality. 'The court always favors the natural mother,' he said. 'You'd be sure to win in a lawsuit. . . .' "

Fortunately Ilse knew better. She was sophisticated enough about adoption to know that a mother does not give up her child on any absurd premise of automatic refund. But she advises girls who are dealing with large agencies to put their hands on as much written material as possible. There was a great deal of help she could have used badly and could have gotten easily if she had only known it existed. It seems clear that too often the people who ostensibly carry an agency's policies to the public do not do a thorough job. Most agencies have a list and explanation of services that are available on request and, as Ilse says, "are well worth wading through" no matter how boring much of the professional jargon is.

Another aspect of pregnancy counseling that irritates people is just that kind of automatic professional rhetoric that blocks out seeing what the needs of an individual client actually are.

June, for example, knew from the beginning that she wanted to keep her child. The only reason she went to an agency was for advice on how to best go about this. But she found herself unable to get through the counselor's view of her as "unmarried mother," which resulted in counseling that was totally irrelevant to June's needs. "It was fantastic," June says. "All this stuff from Sociology 101 pouring out of her without a clue as to what kind of person she was talking to. On and on about how it was 'understandable I should try and make up for my lonely, empty life, but that it wasn't really fair to the baby.' But what really got me," she says with a grin, "was this garbage about how she 'was going to help me pick up the pieces.'" The very repeating of the phrase made June whoop in laughter, and anyone looking at her could understand why. She is a tall, beautiful black girl with the kind of figure that makes other women pull their coats much tighter around them. She works as a copywriter in a major advertising agency where she has been responsible for several nationally successful commercial campaigns. "Pick up what pieces?!" she yells, as she remembers out loud. "I told her, look honey, my life's never been in pieces, and it's never going to be. I don't want to start a new life, I've got a great life right now, and it's going to stay exactly that way. That poor dumb chick," she says smiling, "I threw her whole script right out the window."

The story of pregnancy counseling is not of course all so grim. Most of the time it is truly helpful, and any pregnant girl would be well advised to use her community's counseling resources as much, if as carefully, as possible. Most churches and religious organizations have, or at least can refer a person to, a counseling service. The Department of Social Services in any state will either offer services themselves or refer people to private agencies. In New York City, for example, the city contracts with private agencies, subsidizing the cost for girls who are unable to afford particular programs. The Child Welfare League and Planned Parenthood will advise girls where to go for particular kinds of counseling. YWCAs or YWHAs often have programs geared for the single pregnant girl. Many cities have maternity and infant care projects under the directorship of the United States Children's Bureau that are administered by local health departments. The yellow pages will tell you the name of the county health department, where such programs can be checked out. An interesting contemporary note is that many yellow pages now list a category of Problem Pregnancies. Included in this catchall phrase are the various problems of illegitimate pregnancies, as well as the health problems of legitimate mothers-to-be.

A few words should be said here about the more personal level of counseling—advice from friends and family. Admittedly it is a heavy method of testing friendship, but many girls felt that the old saw, "you find out who your friends are," held true when they revealed the fact they were pregnant. As Ilse said, "Those people who really cared about me seemed to be the ones who urged me to keep the baby. They said things like, 'I know you'll be able to handle it,' and 'it will be good for you to have someone to love.'" She contrasted this kind of advice with that given by people who seemed more motivated to maintain personal value systems, with little regard for what was really best for Ilse. "They were the ones who either advised abortion or adoption, rather abstractly, as a principle they believed in and so arbitrarily, believed in for me."

This attitude was often particularly present in advice that came from a girl's parents. Rarely was a parent able to suspend personal feelings of guilt or disappointment or embarrassment in his or her advice to the daughter. "I knew my mother was only worried about the neighbors," Jo Ann said, while Ilse recalled her mother's fear of what her stern husband would say. "It was sad," Ilse said. "I know she wanted a grandchild terribly, and she's a religious person in the very best sense. Yet she was encouraging me to have an abortion out of fear of my father's response to my having an illegitimate baby. Fortunately I was able to see through her supposedly objective advice, and fortunately too, I didn't need any help from my father financially so I could afford to defy him."

The cost of pregnancy is of course one aspect that worries many single parents. Many girls simply cannot afford the cost of a private obstetrician, which generally begins at around $500. Several girls did find doctors who were willing to lower their fees considerably when they learned there was no husband to subsidize the pregnancy. Interestingly, most obstetricians were more admiring than disapproving of their husbandless patients.

"I was terribly impressed with her," Ilse's doctor says. "You have no idea of how many little girls walk through my door with mommy on one side and the husband on the other, and they're still scared to death about being a mother, or else absolutely unaware of what motherhood really means. A girl like Ilse, who's got it all planned, and is willing to shoulder it all on her own, Christ, how can I feel anything but admiration? I asked her what she could afford to pay, and it came very close to my regular fee. But if it hadn't, I would have delivered her anyway."

Many single women whose physicians' approval did not also affect their fees as Ilse's doctor's did, met obstetrical costs through the Medicaid system. Private medical care is often impossible for anyone not insured by some medical plan, and unmarried pregnancies are not blessed by most large insurance companies. This leaves girls, even those with good-paying jobs, often dependent upon the social service departments of their states for financial aid.

Individual states have different provisions to cover the cost of care under the Medicaid system. At the local level it is administered through the welfare department, although you can receive Medicaid without being on the welfare rolls. Sometimes you are sent to a Medicaid clinic or assigned to a specific doctor, but often you are able to select a private physician and deliver at the private hospital he normally sends his patients to. The Department of Social Services can provide information about applying for Medicaid while also explaining the varied services available to an unmarried mother. In New York City, for example, the Unmarried Parents Programs lists among its services, "prenatal medical care, counseling, guidance, training in the care of children, family planning, vocational guidance," and reports maternity shelter care can be provided when indicated.

The maternity shelter is in fact a possibility for the unmarried mother that she often overlooks. Religious groups and private agencies maintain residential homes for pregnant girls in almost every one of our states. Maternity homes have drastically changed in philosophy and approach since their conception years ago. The "shelter" aspect, a place where girls went to hide their "shame," is almost totally gone, philosophically as well as experientially. And gone along with it is the fact that almost every girl who went to a home ended by giving her baby up for adoption. Now, more and more girls who spend time in maternity homes plan to keep their children. In fact, several places are creating postnatal residences where the single mother can stay on with her baby for a while until she is ready to make more permanent arrangements. The Bureau of Child Welfare can refer a pregnant girl to a maternity home and can explain in detail what services are offered through it.

These homes are not federally or state funded. Therefore, they must support themselves to some extent through the people they service. They do receive money from various community organizations, but this never covers the total cost of their operation. Some fees to clients, consequently, can be quite high, although they generally are set up on a sliding scale. Usually a realistic figure and schedule of payment will be worked out between the social worker and client, based on the client's income and future plans. Today welfare and social service departments often will underwrite these costs, in many cities contracting directly with the home to provide its services for city residents.

Many homes are affiliated with hospitals where the girl can go to work. Figures released in May, 1972, showed that 40 perquestion of hospital costs can loom large as delivery draws near. A figure of $75 a day for a semiprivate room is standard anywhere in the country, with hospitals in large cities asking a great deal more than that. While there are public hospitals that offer clinic care, the private teaching hospital connected with a medical school does the same thing, and generally in a much more pleasant atmosphere. Several girls who had their children in such hospitals found their stays highly satisfactory. They obviously stayed in a maternity ward rather than in a private room, but the atmosphere was congenial and they found the hospital staff supportive and not at all hostile to their social status. Occasionally a particular nurse or intern would come on as a "heavy," but these seemed to be rare occurrences in the experience of becoming a single mother. One girl told about a nurse "draped in rosaries" who kept telling her to get her tubes tied so she would not have any more "fatherless" babies. But even here the woman was more annoyingly hovering than really hostile.

As for dealing with other mothers, this too seemed more a problem in anticipation than it was in the actual experience. On maternity wards, there are always likely to be other unmarried patients, so a single mother will not feel singled out. And girls who were in semiprivate rooms found the other women really too absorbed in their personal dramas to pay much attention to absent father figures on the other side of the room. If the question did come up, a direct response of "I'm not married," seemed to be taken quite easily. On the other hand, some girls like Ilse felt they wanted time alone to feel more comfortable about their new role, and they managed to save while pregnant for the cost of a private room.

"I'm a private person anyway," Ilse said. "And I needed to adjust away from other people's judgments. I even told my friends I didn't want visitors, with just a couple of exceptions. I said to my doctor that I had enough money to pay for four private days in the hospital, and that's all I would stay."

Ilse actually had the only really bad interpersonal experience involved with being a single parent that I heard about. Her baby was born with a birth deformity that required extensive treatment, much of it surgical. The doctor told her the baby would have to stay in the hospital at least a month to have preliminary surgery, the first of many operations she would have in the first few years of her life. The prognosis for complete cure was high, but so were the estimated costs of that cure. The baby was put in an intensive care unit at a pulse-racing rate of $200 a day. She was there for several weeks, and Ilse estimates the bill to be around $5,000. By now, the child's medical expenses are closer to $10,000, and more is still to come.

As soon as they realized the situation, Ilse was advised by her physician to apply for Medicaid. The hospital, a medium-sized, private teaching hospital, had a representative of Medicaid on its staff who came up to talk to her. He kept insisting Ilse supply the name of the baby's father on her application form. Her refusal to do so seemed to infuriate him.

"I had no intention of putting a name down," Ilse says, "so I simply told him I didn't know who the father was. But he just wouldn't accept that. He kept insisting I had to know, how could I not know. We never did resolve it, at least to his satisfaction. I finally told him to put down any name he liked, and he put down John Doe or something, waved the piece of paper in my face and stomped out. Maybe my casualness put him off. Who *knows* why? Perhaps it was something else, but it was really quite unpleasant and I was afraid I wouldn't get the money."

A nurse who had been in the room told Ilse's doctor about the incident. Later that day he came to see Ilse and in her words was "livid" when she confirmed the story. He went immediately to the man and made it loudly clear that he resented his attitude and would not tolerate such an incident happening again. And no further problems did occur. As a matter of fact, Ilse was told that the hospital had, as a number of hospitals do, a fund for subsidizing cases such as hers, and had Medicaid not come through, the hospital would have absorbed her daughter's medical costs.

The question of filling in the father's name is an issue that concerns many single parents, quite apart from medical forms. What do you put on the birth certificate? Leaving the space for father's name blank clearly establishes that the child in fact has no legal father. But putting in the name of the child's natural father is still a different name than your own, and so also indicates you are not married (even though it does seem to suggest an acknowledged relationship between the father and the child). Several girls, some with the man's agreement, others without his being aware of it, did choose to list the real name of the baby's father on the birth certificate. But psychologically, for a child, it is felt that putting down the name of a man who has no intention of ever recognizing his relationship, may be more disturbing than listing no name at all. There are, particularly in such changing times, substantial arguments to be made to a child about why a permanent relationship with the man responsible for his conception was not realistic. But putting down his name can imply more than a casual relationship and so can create, if the father has never been heard from, a feeling of rejection and abandonment.

There is another reason to resist the temptation to fill in a space that looks too jarringly blank. Recent legislation has occurred that gives greater rights to unmarried fathers than have ever been given before. Traditionally the unwed mother had full legal rights to her child. However, the Supreme Court in April, 1972, struck down an Illinois law that severely limited the rights of unwed fathers, granting them now the same rights divorced or widowed fathers would have over their children. This particular case involved a father's custody claim after the natural mother's death, but legal opinion seems to be that the door is open for a variety of cases involving custody rights of the natural unmarried father. A father, who at the time of his baby's birth seemed totally disinterested in the child, might easily change his mind later on. His name listed on the birth certificate would be an important asset to him, should that change of heart occur. It is important, then, that a single mother realize the times are changing all around her. She can no more rest comfortably on old legal definitions of her rights than she can abide by old moral definitions of how she should live her life.

One single mother is currently searching for her seven-year-old daughter whose father simply took her off the street one day. Should the mother locate them, she anticipates a difficult time regaining custody. It is a tragic situation, and she tearfully warns all single mothers to have as much legal awareness as possible to avoid tragedy's touch in their own lives.

Some girls feel the need to pretend marriage. On the birth certificate they either claim to be married to the baby's father or invent a fictitious husband. Again, there is a pragmatic reason for the policy of honesty. If she should ever really marry, and her husband would like to adopt her child, she will have to prove that no such person as her first husband ever existed. Awkward and humiliating as this is, the result of listing the real natural father as a legal husband can be a lot worse. For in this case, unless she can prove they were in fact *not* married, he would have to be located to formally relinquish his rights to the child before adoption could take place.

The birth certificate, then, is not an arena for revenge or apology. The legal documents of our existence follow us through life, and they should be filled out with that in mind. Single mothers who simply filled in their own names seem confident that honesty was the simplest alternative and in the best interests of their children. Seeing parenthood as an independent role, and not as part of an institutional framework, allows these women to feel they can meet future questions from their children head-on. "I'll tell him he has my name, and that's a pretty good one," Jo Ann says. "But what's most important really is going to be what he does with that name. Married or not, a child belongs to you only a very short time. At least that's how I feel. He's an extension of no one. He's an individual who's going to make his own life. If he didn't have the stuff to do that, six names on the damn certificate wouldn't make a difference."

Jo Ann's certainty is, of course, not so completely shared by other single mothers. Many in fact felt a sudden rush of uncertainty for the first time when their babies were about to be born. "As I was being taken down to the labor room," said Ilse, "I had this terrible sense of how irrevocable it was. I wanted to say, 'I changed my mind . . . I can't handle it.' I felt the baby pushing down and knew no matter what I wanted it was going to be born. I was terrified. I had been so sure of myself, but suddenly I wanted so to have my mother there, or anyone, to lean on."

Most girls who have been through the experience strongly recommend that tough, go-it-alone feelings be suspended for the trip to the hospital and the baby's birth. Even without the concept of fear, the important events of life generally are richer when shared.

If a mother, or member of the family, or good friend is available and the kind of person the mother-to-be likes to have around, she (or he) should be asked to share the first hours at the hospital. Most hospitals allow visitors in the labor room, at least for a while. There is little question that time passes faster and with less room for fear when that particular room's space is shared.

After delivery, too, it is nice to have someone around who cares about what has just taken place. To some degree, every new mother experiences emotional upheaval during the postpartum period. Usually, the first news that the baby has been born brings a wave of euphoria. It's over . . . all that waiting . . . the stomach's flat, the mystery of whether it's a boy or girl solved. But with some people, the rising curve of happiness spirals sharply into a downward line, making many women depressed, some severely so. Some opinion has it that postpartum depression is aggravated when a mother is ambivalent about her child. However, it seems that this view usually precludes the single mother as a candidate for the experience.

As one psychologist said, "They've generally been so much closer to their feelings, because they had to do a lot more thinking about motherhood than a married girl does. Usually, by the time the baby's born, they're pretty clear about things. Besides," he added, "they're feeling pretty proud of themselves by that time."

Most of the girls involved with this book seemed to bear out his opinion. The vast majority said they "had never felt better" than during the first weeks after their babies arrived. And they were, indeed, triumphant. There was a sort of self-congratulatory glee, a feeling they had carried off something pretty significant in those months they carried their babies. If they were people who cherished the idea of independence, they felt now more realistically independent than ever before. "When I looked at my son through the nursery window the first day," June recalled, "I had the feeling I had really blessed him with a great power. That he was born in independence and freedom, and the fact that he was, would help shape his life the same way. I stood there looking at him, and I just started to laugh. I wanted to put my hand through the window and grab his hand and say, 'Honey, you and me, we beat the system, you know that?' "

If the system is not beaten, it certainly is being bent into new shapes by girls such as June.

The Single Parent's Family

THE NEWS THAT THEY will be hearing nursery rhymes before a wedding march makes many girls' parents less than thrilled at her plans for their future. Even a woman who is panting to be a grandmother may find this particular route to the role a hard one to travel. It is important to remember that most single parents' parents grew up on the other side of birth control pills, women's liberation, and the myriad other influences that made the idea of single parenthood possible. They are people who were taught by their own parents to see sex as irrevocably linked to marriage, and children a legally sanctioned by-product of that marriage. They were taught that it was their own role as parents to raise children who would live upstanding, decent lives, and they were people who knew, they thought, exactly what it took to live those lives. They were people who gained self-esteem largely from how successful they were as parents. And *successful* was translated to mean how well their children lived up to their own tradition-tinged definitions of success.

To live in a situation where the young lead the way, which is what our contemporary situation is, makes many older people uncomfortable. That yesterday's values are irrelevant can make the person who holds them feel irrelevant and, therefore, defensive. For if they do let go of these once solid codes and admit their faded strength, what can they replace them with at this stage of life? It is difficult for a mother who is certain only "bad" girls become pregnant outside of marriage to accept the news that her unmarried daughter is going to have a child. And if the mother has primarily defined herself these past years by how "good" a mother she is, she may respond to the news not only with anger but with feelings of extreme personal failure.

"I tried so hard," Jo Ann said, "not to have my mother see herself as responsible. I tried to make her see that neither one of us had anything to be guilty about. But she's still living in her own girlhood, and I couldn't make her see how things have changed." Some girls have been willing to soothe their parents' confusion and pain by making up stories in language they could better understand. As soon as she discovered she was pregnant, Edith wrote her parents that she had met a man "who was everything they wanted for me," she recalls. "I really painted him in larger than life colors, so they would eventually be able to understand how I couldn't resist 'temptation.'" After a few weeks she began hinting that they were going to become engaged, and then wrote that indeed they had decided to marry. She even went so far as to discuss bringing him home for a visit on the next holiday weekend. And then, after a few weeks had gone by, she wrote a long, sorrowful letter about how he had jilted her. She went home to be "comforted," and there, in the climate of her mother's wish to support her, she "confessed" that she was pregnant.

"I know it was a pretty elaborate plan," Edith says sheepishly. "But I don't feel I compromised myself or really manipulated my parents. I was just being practical and trying to make things easier for everybody."

Many psychologists agree that Edith's understanding of her

parents' need for rationalization can be important in maintaining relationships at this time. "A girl has to understand that to parents, her behavior is very much a reflection on them," one doctor said. "How their children turn out is a big factor in how they assess their own lives. If the child does something 'deviant,' then their own lives are questioned. Either they failed, or their kid failed them."

Rebecca's parents chose to place the burden of failure on her. How could she have done this to them? After all they had done for her? "It was as if the only reason I had become pregnant was to get back at them for something," Rebecca says wonderingly. "They simply couldn't see me as a separate person with needs that had nothing at all to do with them. It drove me wild!"

What particularly bothered Rebecca is that she began to see her parents in a previously repressed perspective. The fact that they were not able to temper their negative feelings by pleasure at her happiness awoke old resentments. "I always used to think that they only saw me as an object of their needs. I remember as a kid, for example, I used to hate going to sleep-away camp. But my mother brainwashed me that it was good for me to develop skills and self-confidence away from home. Deep down I always felt they just wanted to get rid of me for a while. I'd managed to talk myself out of that attitude when I got older, but when I saw how they reacted to my pregnancy, it opened it all back up, and now no one can convince me that it's my best interests they've really ever had at heart. I'm a parent now," she added, "and I know I want most of all for my daughter to be happy. As long as I felt she *was* happy, I wouldn't care how she found it."

The news of illegitimate pregnancy can in fact bring many quiescent family conflicts to a head. In a crisis situation, defenses are down, and at the same time positions can become rigidly polarized so interaction takes place on a much rawer level. Several girls who had been living in ways their parents tolerated in thin-lipped silence found the silence thunderously broken by their own ultimate statement of self.

"I knew my mother didn't approve of me," Marion says. "I had left graduate school, and then I moved out to my own apartment. But she'd never said anything directly. Until I told her I was pregnant, and then, man, it all hit the fan! Every complaint she'd had about me since I was twelve. It was just awful. And she was almost triumphant," Marion says unhappily. "As if she'd been waiting for an inevitable disaster and at last here it was. I think it kills her that I'm managing so well."

Sometimes the problem is just the reverse. When a daughter is held too highly in her parents' eyes, her fall from grace can leave some really painful emotional debris.

"I was always the perfect one in the family," says Ilse. "My brother and sisters really hated me, and I don't blame them. My parents so obviously favored me. And I was so incredibly goody-goody. Always obedient, top student, always helped around the house. I can't really tell you why I maintained that image, or how it influenced my having a baby, though I obviously know there's some connection. Anyway," she continued, "when I came home and told my parents I was pregnant, they simply couldn't believe it. My father kept insisting I must have been raped, and every time I assured him he was wrong, he got more livid. I remember my brother and sisters who were still at home standing in the hall watching what was going on with such amazed looks on their faces."

Today, Ilse and her parents are still affected by that scene. Her mother and she have pretty well picked up their old relationship, but her father has never forgiven her for not living up to his glorified image of perfection's daughter. His contact with her and his grandchild is minimal. In fact Ilse has never brought her child to his home as it is tacitly understood they would not be welcome. Her mother comes to see Ilse, occasionally accompanied by her husband who sits impassively while the rest of his family behaves as a family. One dividend that has resulted, though, is that Ilse and her brother and sisters have never been closer. They all came to see her in the hospital after she had the baby, and said they were anxious to help. And each one said, she recalled with a smile, that they were happy to see she was a human being after all—for it was hard to be related to a goddess.

When to tell a parent the news is also a troublesome question. If a girl has contact with her parents, she obviously has to let them know before her physical condition lets them discover it on their own. If she lives out of town, it is conceivable that she can hide the truth until the pregnancy is well advanced or even till it is over. A couple of girls chose this after-the-fact method, but most people do not recommend it as an ideal method of communication.

Sheila had her sister tell their mother when she gave birth to her daughter. Until that moment, the older woman had no clue that her daughter, while pursuing a successful career, also happened to be pregnant. "I wanted to write her," Sheila says, "but I kept putting it off and putting it off, and then I guess I just chickened out. I was afraid she'd come rushing down here and I'd get upset at her response, which I figured would be pretty emotional. I had regrets, of course. It would have been nice toward the end to have her here to help and give me some support." Actually Sheila's mother was quite upset that she had not been told the news. She feels in retrospect that she would have handled it reasonably. No one, of course, knows that for sure, and her response to the news that Sheila was going to keep her child does not bear out her claim to equanimity.

It is this particular phase of their communication that is particularly problematic for the potential single parent and her family. Even parents who were able to accept the news of their daughter's pregnancy with relative calm recoiled at the news that she was going to keep her child. The majority of parents assumed she would have an abortion, and many in their "liberation" were even willing to foot the bill. When they were told instead that they could save their money for their grandchild's layette, shock waves surfaced with pent-up fury.

"A lot of these people are trying rather desperately to keep up with the times," a psychologist explains. "Here they are, congratulating themselves about how 'modern' they are, how cool they've been about the news that their daughter's pregnant —then wham—they're hit with the added news that she's going to raise the child as a single parent. And this is more modern than they're ready to be. That they're not ready rubs their faces in how much a part of the past they really still are. It makes them feel silly, and it confuses them."

Many adoptive parents also found resistance to their announcements of impending additions to the family. Betty's parents at first made an obviously difficult attempt to restrain their disapproval of her plan to adopt. But when they discovered their new grandchild was going to be interracial, their stiff composure crumbled. Betty was deeply upset when she discovered months after she had adopted her daughter that her parents still had not told their closest friends that Kathi was of mixed racial background. Similarly, Steve, the adoptive father whose child was in fact white, found his parents had not told his uncles and aunts that Steve had done such a "bizarre" thing as to adopt a son. These people, so steeped in finding esteem from others' approval, did not have the courage to risk that approval by telling the truth about their children. At the same time, not yet receiving outside approval of their children's behavior, they held back from giving it to their children themselves.

While both Steve and Betty found relationships strained during this period, they eventually were able to ease some of the tensions. Primarily this happened because they had the ability to be patient, to slow their steps into the future so their parents could catch up. It meant not meeting anger with anger, but instead with real attempts to help the parents understand their motives for their unusual decisions. "The important thing," says a family counselor, "is to help parents understand that this is not an act against them in any way. Once they can relax and understand that, they can begin to see themselves as grandparents. Until they can stop being defensive, though, they only see this new child as some aberration of their own children. It's up to the single parent to help them relate to the child as grandparents." Mainly they can do this, he said, by being serious about their own roles as parents, and by making it clear that they are anxious to share their child with the grandparents whenever the grandparents are ready to do so.

Perhaps the element that most helps a family to understand their child is not flaunting her defiance of the norm but only declaring her right to diversity, is the growing awareness that their family situation is not so unique after all. Frequently a mother's timid hint at her daughter's life-style opens the flood gates of "confession" from other parents.

Sheila's mother smiles in self-deprecation when she recalls how long she kept Sheila's child a secret.

"I was depriving myself of a grandchild out of fear that I would lose face in the neighborhood. I'll never forgive myself for not letting Sheila bring the baby home for a while like she wanted to do. I'm terribly impressed that she *can* forgive me," she added. "Anyway," she said, "my husband, who was much more sensible than I was, said it was time to cut it out and come to terms with the situation. So Sheila finally came home, and in the course of preparing my friends and neighbors for her visit, I discovered that there were a couple of divorces in their own children's lives; that one son was in prison in Spain on a drug charge when I thought he was studying; and that one girl was living on a commune with a man old enough to be her father. Here we'd all been playing the game of being so conventional, everyone like everyone else. Well," she said ruefully, "we *were* just like each other, but mainly in that we all felt we were the only one who was different."

It is not easy for people such as Sheila's mother to suddenly find that their parental authority is replaced by uncertain apology for being "old-fashioned." It does help to know others are equally uneasy about their footing in the rapidly changing world. But what helps even more is understanding from a child, in this case the single parent, of just how difficult it is to change moralities in mid-cultural stream. Pushing parents headfirst into that stream does not generally teach them to swim. A little gentleness is called for, and an attempt to recognize how frightening these contemporary waters can seem to someone unfamiliar with them. Dr. Spock, in talking about how grandparents generally have difficulty accepting changing ideas in child care, explained how really hard it is to accept ideas that are totally contradictory to what you yourself learned. Particularly when you were taught that the results of the behavior were not only "bad" but maybe dangerous. He wrote of trying to sympathize with the older generation's alarm at the new, by imagining what our own response might be if, for instance, we were advised to give a brand-new baby a first meal of fried pork, or bathe him in icy cold water!

There is more reason than altruism for a single parent to help her own parents adjust to her decision. Children are often enriched by their relationships with grandparents. A single parent who recognizes her child as a person with independent needs should be aware of this; even if she herself feels she could do quite well without her parents' active presence in her life. Her child, as a child with only one parent, can gain considerable extra security from knowing there is another parental figure to depend on. And even the most independent single parent often welcomes the special kind of assistance that comes from someone who has a family tie to her child. A child who is left with a warm, loving grandparent while his parent takes a vacation, is generally much happier than the one who is left with hired help, no matter how competent they are. Sheila left her daughter with her mother for a two-week trip to Europe, something she could not have contemplated doing without her.

"I know it would have been possible," she says. "But I know myself well enough to know I wouldn't have been relaxed about things without knowing she was with someone who really loved her. And by now, my mother does really love her."

The majority of grandparents do come to love their new lifestyle grandchildren. Ilse's mother is deeply grieved at the joy her husband is missing by his stubborn refusal to accept an "illegitimate" child into his life.

"He loves babies, and he always adored Ilse. I know he's going to regret this period very much later on. And he's being so unfair for such an ethical man. Ilse's baby didn't ask to be born. Why should she be deprived of a grandfather when she, without a father, needs one so particularly? Just because my husband disapproves of how Ilse chose to bring her into the world."

The role of the grandfather in a fatherless family *is* of course important. As is a grandmother to the boys who are the sons of single fathers. They are obviously consistent role models of the opposite sex. But both sex grandparents are also people who can give a child a kind of joyous vacation from many of childhood's problems. Grandparents are generally better able to enjoy their grandchildren than they could their own children. Parents are often so involved with the responsibilities of raising a child, that they miss some of the really great pleasures involved. But a grandmother, without the sometimes oppressive awareness that she is shaping a child's destiny, is freer to enjoy the relationship. Grandparents are often much more tolerant of misbehavior than a parent is or, again, than they ever were with their own children.

However, not all grandparents enjoy being a grandparent on this relaxed level. With a single parent there is always the danger, and it is a very real one, that the grandparent will become too involved with the grandchild. I have cited one case already where a grandmother totally took over her illegitimate grandchild, raising him as if she were his real mother. If a single mother is quite young, the temptation to give in to this other "mothering" is particularly strong. But most, if not all of the time, the motivation of both parent and grandparent is encrusted with neurotic needs that promise to distort all the family relationships. A single parent, then, who wants to have grandparents in her child's life, must be extremely clear about how far that role should extend.

"This doesn't mean a mother or father has to be defensive or restrict the grandparent," a psychologist said. "It only means that the parents should be very clear that they have primary responsibility for their child. They must rely on their own feelings about what is best for him, being open enough, of course, to accept good advice from their parents. I guess," he concluded, "that's really my primary advice. To clarify your own feelings both about being a parent and about being your parents' child. That way you can interact without defensiveness or dependency."

This is a tall order. The ways in which parents and children trouble each other are exquisitely complex. But if single parents are trying to shape new kinds of relationships with their children, then they should be willing to reshape their relationships with their own parents.

Like everything else in this time of reexamination, it opens up excitingly new and plausible ways of experiencing one another within a family.

Child Care

ONE DAY, the realities of being a single parent begin. Papers have been signed, candy has been left for obstetrical nurses, good-byes are said to other patients or adoption caseworkers. The door closes behind parent and child in the apartment or house, and the future is now, and all up to them. What happens now? Do mommy (or daddy) and their new son (or daughter) live happily ever after? The new parent begins to realize that whether they do live happily ever after depends very much on how she can deal with the day-to-day realities of raising a child.

"I had this romantic idea of a clean baby lying in a crib while I painted, never making a sound but a soothing occasional coo. God, was I in for a shock," Elizabeth says. "I had a commission to finish when we came home from the hospital, and I spent nearly my whole fee on baby-sitters who rocked the baby every time she cried so I wasn't distracted by her screeching. It was horrible!"

Elizabeth continues to be frustrated by the demands of motherhood. She feels, as many other single parents do, that much of her anger and, in her case, regret over being a single parent has to do with money. It is an ironic note to this story of antiestablishment morality that the most establishment symbol of all figures so importantly in a single parent's life. Men and women who have abandoned middle-class worship of the dollar find themselves worrying about where the next dollar will come from, and how to make the dollar they do have stretch to its furthest possible point.

"I really think if I had enough money I could enjoy being a mother," Elizabeth says. "I could hire the right kind of help or send her to a private nursery school. I used to make fun of my parents for talking so much about money, and now I'm practically obsessed by it. If I'm not talking about art, I'm talking about money. That's why I won't take a job," she explains, looking at me intensely. "I know the temptation to prostitute my talent for a good salary would be too great. So I won't work in the art department of an advertising agency or something like that. I'd rather take these part-time jobs as a studio helper or even a waitress, and at least know I only paint at a level I can be honest about."

Elizabeth's determination to pursue her career purely, adds greatly to her problems. She is on welfare, but because she spends so much on art supplies, and wants to maintain her larger-than-necessary apartment so she can have some privacy to paint, she has little money left over. The day-care setups in her neighborhood are inadequate as they are in most neighborhoods. Private baby-sitting is just about impossible.

"I had some old biddy from down the street taking Ellen out to the park a couple of hours so I could work," she says. "One day it started to rain, and they didn't come back, so I went out to look for them. I found my daughter playing in the sandbox, which now, of course, was all soppy and muddy. She was covered with mud. It was even dripping into her face, because she had put sand in her hair, and the rain was washing it down over her eyes. As I pulled her out, it started to thunder and lightning. Neither of us was dressed for the rain, and she was smearing me all over with her mud and kicking and crying. I started to cry too, it was so nightmarish. The goddamn sitter was nowhere to be found. That night she called me up and said Ellen had wandered off and she'd gone to look for her, and then got confused about where they'd really been sitting. I'll bet she was confused," Elizabeth finished bitterly. "She probably was sitting in the local bar boozing up. Well, that was the end of my 'bargain' baby-sitter. Regular prices I could never afford."

Elizabeth's welfare caseworker is actually sympathetic to her dilemma. She receives a total of $225 a month from the city. Her rent is $148 a month, and she feels another counselor might well have pressured her to move to a cheaper apartment; as she might also be pressured into taking a job now that her daughter is older. But still another interesting aspect of a culture in change is that change often occurs on an individual level inside the most entrenched institutions. Agencies such as the welfare departments of many large cities will often have employees interpreting the agency's philosophies in radically contemporary terms.

"I was really worried about that first interview," Elizabeth remembers. "I had the image of some old biddy in tennis shoes sniffing around me in disapproval. Instead I got this real swinging guy who is just as anxious to beat the system as I am. I mean he's not ripping them off or anything. He just believes that you shouldn't make people crawl because they need some help."

The welfare mother image is, however, one that still haunts much of society and Elizabeth finds it hard not to be belligerent about her desire to stay on its rolls.

"Even my own parents are disapproving," she says. "And every once in a while you meet one of those creeps who tell you they're really supporting you by their taxes. Once I met a guy at a party, and he took me and Ellen home—of course, I *always* have to bring her to parties. He came up here and practically raped me after I tried to turn him down nicely. And he actually told me I owed it to him because he was supporting us if we were on welfare."

Rebecca is a welfare mother who feels no sense of indignity. Of course, she has none of Elizabeth's frustrations about wanting success in a career. Rebecca is one of the few natural mothers I talked to who really planned her baby in a long-term way. And her decision to be on welfare is based simply on a desire to be with her daughter as much as possible. For this expression of "mother love" she has no apology.

"Why should I go to work and leave her to prove how responsible a citizen I am?" she asks, flashing a marvelous big smile. "I know where my responsibilities are. They're to her," and she points to her baby lying in her borrowed playpen.

Everything Emily owns is either borrowed or a gift. Proudly, Rebecca will tell you that she had to buy nothing for her daughter. All baby equipment, and all her clothing were either outright presents or are shared on a rotating basis among friends with children. Rebecca lives in a one-bedroom apartment on the suburban edges of an eastern city. It is a neighborhood that once held many more families than it does now. Rebecca's building, however, still is home to many older couples who remained there after their children moved away. Yet no one in the building, she feels, is anything but delighted with the new life-style in apartment 3B.

"Just last week," Rebecca says, "while my caseworker was still here, a lady from upstairs whom I'd never really spoken to came to see me. She had this huge bundle in her arms. She wanted to just drop it and leave when she saw June, my counselor, but I insisted she stay and have coffee with us. Then I opened the package, and you can't believe it. There were dozens of baby clothes, each piece wrapped up separately in Saranwrap. They looked fresher and better quality than anything you see in any store. Honestly!" While she was talking, she pulled open a drawer and showed me the stacks of clothing. "See?" she says, beaming. "That's only part of it, can you believe it? She told me they were her daughter's clothing, and she'd been saving them all these years hoping her daughter would have children of her own. But she hasn't yet, so when she saw me come home from the hospital with the baby, she just decided to let them be used while they could. And do you know what that darling woman said when she left? 'I hope you're not insulted.' Insulted! I think it's so beautiful a person would do that . . . so beautiful!"

Rebecca's joyous response to motherhood reflects her long period of preparation for the role. She is totally enthusiastic about single parenthood, considering herself a "real advocate" of the experience. She believes that people who think they would like to "try it" should not hold back, should not remain childless and frustrated because of doubt or fear. On the other hand, she believes it is a decision to be "thought out" in very concrete ways.

"You can't just go ahead and get pregnant because you think it would be nice to have a baby around the house," she says. "The financial security that I have has made all the difference to me." She told of a friend who had no such security and ended up, like Elizabeth, often deeply resenting her baby for the enormous burdens it placed on her life.

"She was a nice Jewish girl from the suburbs," Rebecca says with a laugh, "just like I am. Only she believed that nice Jewish girls from the suburbs don't go on welfare. I know better."

Of course, as Rebecca indicates, welfare alone would not have made this first year as problem free as it has been so far. Two years ago, as soon as she decided she wanted a baby, Rebecca began saving her money. "I'd always spent every dime I earned, but as soon as the decision was made, I became an absolute miser."

The father of Rebecca's baby is now gone, but he and Rebecca lived together for those two years. She always beseeched him to make her pregnant, although she did not want any commitment from him for the future. Their lives were moving in different paths, and neither one blamed the other for what they knew would be an eventual parting.

"He was into a whole film-making thing. He really wanted to travel and be a documentary producer. I just wanted to weave a little and stay home. I couldn't really fit into the life he planned for himself; I couldn't and I didn't want to."

But she kept prevailing on Don, her lover, to give her a baby. She wanted to have a child with someone she loved. Finally, "as a birthday present," she says laughing, he did do his part in her master motherhood plan. Rebecca conceived on the night of her birthday; which adds fuel to the adoption worker's view that there are emotional dynamics to conception. Rebecca herself is less psychological than mystical about the on-target timing of her daughter's conception.

Nonetheless, in a very nonmystical fashion, to the money she had already saved in anticipation of Don's agreeing to be a father she added during her pregnancy money saved from two full-time jobs. She worked as an arts and crafts teacher during the day at a local nursery school and as a waitress in the evening. This particular combination of jobs allowed her even to save on food costs, as she had lunch with the children, and the restaurant gave her dinner. She had estimated what it would cost her to live, on welfare, for at least a year without working, and by the time Emily was born she had reached her goal with a little extra besides.

In many ways Rebecca's life has never been freer from the variety of problems getting or keeping a dollar can bring. For openers, this is the first time in her adult life that she has not had a full-time job. She revels in her new freedom from schedule, loves being able to nap when the baby does. Not working means she saves money on clothes. She doesn't need "outside grown-up clothes," wearing her handwoven blouses and old jeans around the apartment, or when she takes the baby out for a walk. She has none of the commuting expenses those who earn their daily bread have to pay for that privilege. Her food expenses are minimal. She breast-feeds Emily, and she herself is a disciple of simple eating. Her diet leans toward rice and cereals with almost no meat, out of preference more than pennypinching. The $225 she, like Elizabeth, receives from welfare covers her $104-a-month rent and leaves about $25 extra a week. To this, with her counselor's discreet look the other way, she adds another $25 each week by doing one day of typing for a magazine she once worked for. Usually she can do the typing at home. If there's an emergency and she has to go to the office, she either leaves Emily with a baby-sitting friend or takes her along.

Both these child-care alternatives are frequently part of the single parent's alternative life-style. The flexibility they showed in assuming the role of single parent pervades the way they behave as single parents. In a time when people are often painfully separating themselves from certainties and absolutes, many single parents seem to suffer little anxiety about the separation process. They are comfortable with uncertainty and unafraid of ambiguity. Not all are, of course. But for those parents who, like Rebecca, combine cool reason with emotional independence, there is a remarkable ability to roll with life's punches and make life do some of the adjusting. Like Rebecca, many single parents have worked out cooperative baby-care arrangements with friends, but they are also willing to welcome the most unlikely person into the category of friend when baby-sitting is necessary.

Hear June on this. "I've been shopping in this momma/poppa grocery store for years, and after the baby came, they really were still very nice to me. So a couple of times, when I've had an emergency, I just took her down there in her carriage and asked if they'd look out for her. Now I think they wait for me to have a reason to leave her."

Or this from Maryann, a mother who is not on welfare but works at a full-time modeling job. "I have a really good housekeeper, but once last month she was sick for over a week. Three days I took the baby to work with me, but then I had to go on location all day and it would have been too much for him. So I left him with my favorite photographer. I called Charlie and asked if I could leave him for the afternoon, and he said sure. I gave his secretary instructions about feeding him, but when I came to pick Danny up, she said her boss never let her get near him all day. And when I walked into the studio expecting to see Danny asleep in his carriage, I found

Charlie had him in the darkroom, slung over his back in an improvised sling. Danny had the best time of his life," she says happily.

A particular thread connects many single parents in the area of child care—a fascinating combination of openness, ingenuity, and a willingness to invite other people into their often engagingly flexible life-styles. So much of the nuclear families' isolated operations are based on a fear of "losing face." They have a horror of "imposing," or of stepping over the line of accepted social behavior.

The single parent more often than not has left all these attitudes behind. Honesty, if not the best policy, is better than hypocritical service to good form. Like the poet who does not say a poem is "good" or "bad" but only if "it works," the single parent rarely stops to judge whether the behavior he is considering is proper or improper but only if it is possible. To the more timid traveler into tomorrow, it is amazing how so much does indeed turn out to be "possible."

Ilse had made a quite conventional arrangement early in her pregnancy for a visiting exchange student to care for her baby when it arrived. Everything fit together neatly, the girl's college classes and Ilse's working hours. But neatness did not count in Ilse's story, because her baby was born with birth defects that required surgery, and she felt full-time motherhood was called for. She took a leave of absence from her job as executive assistant to a department chairman in a large urban university, telling her boss she would return in early spring. Her boss unhappily agreed, but during the three-month period of the baby's surgery and recuperation, the student became impatient, and took another job.

"I tried to get someone else to care for her," Ilse says, "but it was absolutely prohibitive. Through a private employment agency, the minimum salary for a baby nurse is about $85 a week. If I wanted someone like a retired nurse with real experience, the salary was closer to $150. Well, that was just out of the question."

On the morning of April 2, the day Ilse was due back at

work, she left for her job with her daughter under her arm. Her boss had been away on a trip and she hadn't been able to reach him beforehand to tell him her plans.

"So that morning I just showed up and said, 'Look, it's both of us or none of us,' and he said, 'Well, let's try it.'"

And so the first year of her daughter's life was spent in the English department of a major university. Perhaps it was the impressively academic atmosphere, but the baby responded to her environment with what Ilse's employer seriously tells you was "great dignity." In a corner of Ilse's small private office a portable crib-playpen was set up, and there the baby played and slept while business went on quite as smoothly as it had before. The baby was, according to Ilse, "loved by everyone," and now that she is older and having other kinds of care, her occasional visits to the office are major events for the entire staff. As you enter Ilse's boss's office, by the way, there are two pictures prominently displayed. One is of himself and the president of the university. The other is of the baby sitting on his lap and trying to grab his glasses.

When you talk to the professor about this rather unique arrangement, he quite tersely brushes away his own part in its success. He says only that Ilse is a remarkably efficient person and that she managed to fit the baby's needs into her own work schedule so that no one suffered. But other people in the office very much connect him with Ilse's ability to combine motherhood and a career. What is more, they say that their opinion of the man changed markedly because of it.

"We were always intimidated by him," one girl said. "He's a brilliant man but, well . . . forbidding. . . ." An assistant professor in the department called him "stuffy," and someone else, "cold." They use these words in the past tense, however.

"They say," says Ilse, "that they never expected that from him. And I," she finishes, sounding surprised, "never expected anything else."

Ilse's expectation that her boss would respond well to the unexpected is not an act of arrogance. It is again that resilient openness that is so typical of many single parents. A psychologist I talked to applauded the idea that people such as Ilse are leading less certain paraders away from convention's lockstep. "We're much too quick to think other people aren't ready to go along with change. They may not be ready to take the initiative yet," he said, "but they're often very ready, in fact eager, to follow along."

Certainly this seems to be true as one looks at how single parents are fitting their life-styles into the life that surrounds them. Jo Ann takes her baby regularly to her office on the days of his clinic checkup, as the clinic is in the same neighborhood as her job. The advertising agency she works for is one of the leading agencies in the world, and her boss is considered one of the industry's toughest women. But at least once a month, Jo Ann's son sleeps in a huge file drawer in her boss's office where displays are generally kept, or plays contentedly on the floor, nestled in the luxury of a vice-president's mink coat. Other copywriters are no longer surprised to find Eric perched on their director's lap when they bring an ad in for her approval. "She's no less bitchy about our work," one man told me, "but we get a kick out of seeing her in a more human light. We're all really fond of her and respect her . . . but it's always nice to know the gods have real blood in their veins."

Actually, several other working mothers in Jo Ann's office are grateful to Jo Ann for leading the way down paths that are making their own lives much easier. Many girls now bring their children to work when baby-sitting arrangements fall through, something they never would have considered doing before Jo Ann made the idea plausible.

"It would *never* have occurred to me, *ever*," a married research assistant told me. "My husband is in business for himself, and I can't tell you how many times he's worked at home instead of the office because our sitter conked out; and I, of course, had to work at the office or else not work at all. But more than that," she said rather wonderingly, "it's had an incredible spiraling effect. My husband was horrified when I told him I was bringing Jenny with me the first time. He couldn't wait until dinner time to see how it went. When he heard it was

OK for me, and absolutely groovy as far as she was concerned, he was astounded. But now, *his* secretary does the same thing. She called in one day to say she couldn't come to work because her daughter's nursery school was closed because of a heating problem, and he said, 'Bring her along!' Now he says some of his associates are doing the same thing, since they see it working for him. I told Jo Ann she's started a goddamn revolution!"

Jo Ann, or other single parents, cannot be given total credit for the surprisingly relaxed climate behind our corporate doors. Our societal attitudes about child care have drastically changed these last ten years. Men are asking to play a much more active role in raising their children, and women are saying, "It's about time."

The idea that any kind of maternal separation automatically means a child will be seriously deprived is also being overturned. Early research into institutionalized children showed serious emotional problems resulting from a lack of loving care. In our never-ending fondness for sweeping generalizations, the conclusion was made that children needed constant maternal attention for emotional health. We equated all separations of mother and child in the same way. A mother who took a two-week vacation without her child was properly guilty—every sign of discontent her child exhibited for the next six months she would blame on herself. And as far as having a full-time career, these were Walter Mitty fantasies to be kept, like other aberrations, to oneself.

But the age of generalization is over. There are legitimate arguments now raised for countless, and often contradictory, positions, and each person must choose for himself.

More and more mothers, married and not, are choosing to go to work. Figures released in May, 1972, showed that 40 percent of the jobs in New York City were held by women. Nationally, statistics tell similar stories. The single mother has separated being a mother from being a wife. But married as well as single mothers are questioning whether being a mother is really a synonym for being a person.

There is increasing dissatisfaction with having to answer the cultural roll call as only "Julie's mommy"; and nowhere is this more apparent than in the chaotic problems suddenly facing our nonmommy child-care systems. Most other cultures provide well-run day-care facilities for their working mothers. In America, where most male legislators have self-righteously held back funds believing a mother's place is in the home, there are few such institutions. But one professional magazine recently wrote that the 1970s may go down in history as "the decade when day care came into its own in this country."

Day care in our society has traditionally been relegated to the poor. Mothers who had to work were forced to put up with all kinds of generally inadequate facilities for their children. Emphasis was on custodial, rather than developmental, care. This meant that large numbers of children could be herded together under one roof, with just enough people around to see that no one bashed someone else's head open and everyone ate his assembly-line-served meals.

One of the less attractive aspects of our culture is that our problems are often faced only when they begin to touch the middle class. People in drug rehabilitation, for example, are often bitter that only when drugs moved out of the ghetto and into suburbia did legislators start to deal with the problems. The same, in many ways, seems to be true of day care. Now that women's liberated consciousness is demanding liberation from full-time motherhood, society has to provide ways to make this possible and, suddenly, custodial care is not enough.

On a federal level, although there is much arguing about which bill or plan is most desirable, the swell for funding good day-care centers is on. State and city agencies are accelerating efforts to provide more and better services for children of working mothers (or fathers responsible for their child's care). The majority of Model Cities programs, for example, place child-care issues as a "priority concern."

Still, the single mother, like the married mother, is caught in the lagging currents of a culture in transition. The need is here, but the services have yet to catch up. In New York City alone it is estimated that 228,000 children under five years old are "potential users of day care," but there is space for only 64,000 in the city's public and private preschool programs. And in actual fact, New York City has more day-care services than any other city in the country. For this reason, many cities look the other way when independent groups start their own facilities that do not meet every legal requirement for licensing. One group of single parents, along with some married friends, started such a co-op arrangement on their own.

"If I'd waited until they officially opened something up in my neighborhood, I'd never have gotten out of the house," Edith said. Under her leadership, ten mothers now take care of fourteen children five days a week on a rotation basis. This meant that each mother had to go on a four-day-a-week work schedule.

"Three girls had to drop out of the original group, because their jobs didn't make this possible. But we found ten of us who could swing it. We operate as a team, because it's just too many children to handle on your own from eight-thirty to five-thirty. Occasionally, of course, one of the team gets sick or something, and that's another reason for having two people assigned to the job. At least we can carry on—even though the girl who does is ready to be carried out on a slab when the day's over!"

This particular image of fatigue has special significance, for although they tried at first to work from their homes, they found it a really inadequate arrangement for the children's needs. So the group rented a local funeral parlor, complete with leftover caskets that the children play on.

"We had them all soldered closed so that no one could get trapped inside, but I guess it's still rather macabre-looking to see kids sitting on top of a casket, eating a jelly sandwich and coloring. Saves furniture, though," she says with a smile.

Some of the people who have raised an eyebrow at the unorthodox "homes away from home" are representatives of various city agencies who will regularly serve notice that there are violations of certain building and safety codes. Most of the laws are irrelevant and calcifying with age, but they are on the books, and Edith's group, as many others, could at any time be forced to suspend operation. Edith says they do not have the money to make many of the corrections, so are operating "existentially." "We just hope each day that they won't close us up. Our lawyer advised us to hang on and negotiate as best we could on each point, stalling for time, and that's what we do. As long as it lasts, it's a way out of our child-care problems."

Many single parents are using their usually available ingenuity and determination to find solutions for nonavailable "official" day care. Most of the time, as with Edith's group, it involves sharing responsibilities with other parents in the same boat.

One such arrangement literally began in a boat. A single father in the Boston area summered on Cape Cod. Although there were high school girls in the area for baby-sitting, Herb, the father, felt uncomfortable about leaving his seven-year-old son every day with only a teen-ager while he commuted to work. Yet he wanted the boy to have the delights of the beach during the hot weather. One weekend, just before school ended, he and his son were sailing on the Cape and passed another sailboat with a young woman and a little boy about Teddy's age inside it. Sailing alongside each other, Herb discovered she was a recent widow who felt she and her son could use a summer together in new surroundings. The two boys talked and swam together that day, and by the time they were all having dinner together, it was arranged that the mother, Ruth, would take care of Teddy during the day while Herb went to work, an arrangement she felt would be as beneficial to her still-grieving son as for Herb and Teddy.

"In exchange," Herb said, "I spent most of the weekends with the boys. It gave the other boy a male figure around, and it gave Ruth a chance to move out of full-time motherhood and have a little social life of her own. It was a great summer for everybody. I'm trying hard to find a similar arrangement for the city during the winter."

It *is* often difficult to replicate some of the casual child-caring arrangements country or even suburban communities can provide in city life. Ginger moved to an urban commune because she could not stand the loneliness of being a single parent in a large city. If she were not so happy with her friends she would have left the city completely because she feels an urban environment simply is not geared to raising a child. Her first apartment was not near a park and, she says, "I'd have to push the stroller down broken sidewalks back and forth to get my daughter some air. Then when she started walking, she wouldn't sit in the stroller, and God, that was really horrible! I'd constantly be chasing her away from the curb or pulling her out of dog gook." The brownstone she shares now with her commune has a large backyard, and her daughter and the other children are quite content to play within its walled boundaries.

"I'd love for her to really run free, but this is better than having her just run wild. And I'm not exhausted all the time. Do you realize," she asked me, "that there are no places to really sit down in most cities? I mean unless you're in a park, you could walk for blocks and blocks and never find a place to rest. And bathrooms!" Her voice rises again. "Do you know what it's like to have a small kid need to go to the bathroom in the middle of a city? This city wasn't meant for a kid's bladder, believe me!"

Statistics were recently released that showed many more single people are choosing to live in suburban settings than they have ever done before. The pull of the city's excitement for unattached men and women has dimmed a bit. Single parents, just as people without children, are finding, often to their own surprise, that they can live more comfortably among more traditional family units in traditional neighborhoods. Many suburbs are integrating apartment houses into areas of one-family homes, but most of these buildings are a far cry from the steel-and-glass coldness of their "downtown" counterparts. The suburban apartment building will often hold a swimming pool and tennis courts, and community recreation rooms—all wonderful arenas for a single parent and child to extend their family life to other people.

"I know if I'm late from work and my sitter has to leave," one mother said, "I can have her leave my son in the 'rec' room and there are bound to be other kids there for him to play with until I get home. I know he's safe in the building, or even if he should go outside it. When I lived in the city, I was scared to death to have him out of my sight. He had to be watched every minute. It wasn't good for him or me."

Also, she explained, since life among the building's residents is much less formal than in city apartment living, she's comfortable about having her son knock on a neighbor's door or asking herself whether the neighbor would like to exchange baby-sitting.

"It's cheaper, of course, this way; but it's also better, not so impersonal for a child. No one's being 'hired' to take care of him," she said.

City or country, and even when the baby-sitting is paid for, having someone physically close for baby-sitting is a great asset.

When Jo Ann's son was born, she made an arrangement with a woman to care for the baby. The woman, however, would only sit in her own home, which was almost two miles (in city blocks) from where Jo Ann lived.

"It was ridiculous," Jo Ann says. "The woman was nice enough, but dragging the baby and all his equipment there every day was impossible. It was really too far to walk, and such a production getting in and out of a cab. And if the weather was bad, I'd worry about his being outside. One night I came home from work and it was beginning to get dark and had started to rain—I made up my mind when I dragged the carriage down the stairs that this was it. No more! If I had to stay home until I found it, I'd just have to make a better arrangement." That night, exploring several possibilities, she thought of a woman in her building who had three children, two who were school age. The woman had been "curiously" friendly with Jo Ann during her pregnancy. She herself had married young and could not imagine, she said, any life other than being married and a mother. Her greatest regret was that she had had to have a hysterectomy after her last child, and she and her husband were seriously thinking of adopting other children to compensate for what they considered their "loss."

Like the cartoon light bulb flashing "Aha!" Jo Ann called her friend and asked if she would be interested in caring for her baby while she went to work. "Her husband is a city employee, and I knew she could use a few extra dollars. But more importantly, I just knew instinctively that she'd really like to do this kind of work, and so of course the baby would do well there. I don't care what you pay someone. If they don't really like kids, it shows."

Jo Ann's instincts were right. The woman welcomed her surrogate son into her life five days a week with as "motherly" an embrace as any child could want. For Jo Ann, it is as simple an arrangement as the other was complicated. Their apartments are on the same floor, "so it's just a question of walking down the hall. And she has my key if I forget something or the baby needs anything. And I pay her only $25 a week. She absolutely refuses to take any more. Believe me, for the peace of mind she gives me, if I could afford it, I'd give her five times that."

It is not easy to find individual child care for $25 a week, but it is even harder to find people who really are good at the job. There are women, however, even in these activist days, who, like the woman in Jo Ann's story, really like to take care of children. Recognizing this, federal and state programs are creating what may be the most important answer to our day-care needs. Many single parents, particularly mothers of young babies, had their needs met through a program called family day care. For years informal baby-sitting arrangements have been made by working mothers in the homes of friends or neighbors. But with the growing demand for child-care services, attempts are being made to organize these arrangements and to supervise their operations.

Women are selected by city agencies to be surrogate mothers of up to six children in their own homes. They are paid for each child's care, the payment shared on a sliding scale basis by the city and the mother. The homes are licensed to be day-care centers in the same way that larger centers are, and inspected to see if they continue to meet the licensing criteria. Many people feel, for pragmatic and psychological reasons, that this kind of child-care arrangement may be the future for really good day care. It truly moves out of the old custodial model, offering an atmosphere to children that experts believe is vital, especially with the children are very young. "They need to get out of that institutional framework," one supervisor said. For a baby, this kind of care gives one continuing mothering presence in a noninstitutional setting. For an older child who is in school, it is a root, a base for him even when his mother is working. A child needs a place to come "home" to. To have a refrigerator to open instead of regular routinized snacks, to have a soft chair instead of lined-up rows of every chair the same size.

Mothers of young babies, of course, are particularly benefited by this form of day care, as babies are rarely eligible for larger centers. Ilse had to take her daughter to work because at the time she was born even family day care was available only when the child was nearly a year old. Now this has been changed in most cities to two months, and many single mothers are happily becoming part of the program. In New York City, there are at this writing still many available day-care homes for parents who need them, and as interest in the concept grows, there is reason to feel cities throughout the country will increase their own offerings of similar services.

Ilse's daughter was thirteen months old when she first went to a day-care home. After a year of being taken to work with her mother every day, obviously she did not like the idea of being dropped off while her mother dropped out of sight for eight hours.

"The first week it was horrible," Ilse recalls. "I had talked to the day-care mother several times and brought her to her apartment to play. But the first five days I actually left her, she cried continuously."

The social worker in the family day-care program who was assigned to Ilse's "case" met with Ilse and the day-care mother at their request.

"We were kind of deadlocked," Ilse says. "She felt like a failure, and I felt guilty, so both of us were defensive with each other. Yet both of us had good feelings about each other and really wanted to make it work."

Sitting down together with the social worker helped. Ilse had earlier been making suggestions to her part-time counterpart about what might make her daughter happier. "I remember I would say things like, 'She should have her shoes taken off when she naps.' The woman was furious. 'Do you think I *wouldn't* take her shoes off?' she asked me. 'Do I have to be told something like that?' " Ilse repeated their conversation with a smile. She explained to the woman then that she hadn't meant to be insulting, but was only trying to be as explicit as she could about the baby's needs.

"And some mothers *do* put their babies to bed with their shoes on," Ilse said. "I don't think it's such a sin; it's only a way of doing something that wasn't my way and maybe would have confused her. What I was really trying to do was get the woman to know 'our way,' but she thought I was being critical of her intelligence. We got all of this out at our meeting—look, it takes time for two people to adjust to each other, and when there's a baby involved, well, obviously it's going to be that much more complicated."

Recognizing this, they dealt with their differences and agreed to try and stick it out a little longer. If a day-care home proves unsatisfactory for any reason, the parent is helped to find another home, and guidance by a caseworker is always available. In Ilse's case, the group meeting cleared the air enough for time to do the rest. Her daughter has been there almost a year now, and both Ilse and she relate to the day-care apartment and the family it contains as significant extensions of their own home and family life. Single parents who are interested in this kind of day care for their children should contact the social service departments of their city. Even a parent whose salary rated him to pay full costs for this sort of program, would still be paying much less than comparable private child-care arrangements would involve.

There are many indications that the culture is catching up with the reality child-care needs of its individual members. Alert looks into almost any corner of the country will show rethinking taking place about what a child's needs are in relation to outside care. And as this rethinking takes place, steps are being taken to upgrade the quality and forms of such care.

In southern California, a family center exists, funded by a philanthropic organization, that has single parent families living in an apartment complex that is also home to single people without children, married couples, two-parent families, and older people. Any parent trying to raise a child alone is eligible for the program. The apartments are modestly priced. But even more important are the other services the center provides. There is full-time day care in a separate building within the complex. From 6:30 A.M. to 6:30 P.M. Monday through Friday, a child will be cared for. Additionally, the center provides counseling services for parent and child, classes for both along with group meetings of special interest to their community, and job training for single parents who are trying to rethink or focus careers.

Obviously this small oasis for a single parent is not the answer to the needs of growing numbers of single parents. But it is one more indication of the culture's recognition that these needs do in fact exist.

Once again, the single parent may be a metaphor for how many parents, male and female, single or married, are relating today to the role of parent. Because the majority of single parents obviously need outside help and support for their roles, they may lead other parents to consider whether they, too, want more help for their own parent-child needs. The combined voices are causing society to listen as it perhaps has never done before. Industry, for example, is increasingly attracted to establishing day-care centers for its employees. Other companies who do not actually have their own centers sometimes take the lead in starting centers in the communities in which their businesses are located. They will help fund a center's beginnings, or sometimes finance smaller family day-care projects. And still other companies will subsidize an employee's use of already existing day-care services.

Meanwhile, the behaviorists and teachers hurry to update thinking of the role of surrogate child care. "Arguing on the advisability of day care is like arguing the advisability of growing older, we have very little choice in the matter," one psychologist told me. "Family styles are changing, mothers are working in and out of marriage, fathers are raising children on their own. We *have* to supply the ways for them to do this. The question is not *should* we do it, but *how* we should do it."

The big issue in *how* is, of course, what the child's real needs are. Although it is generally acknowledged that children do not have to be with their mothers all the time, it is agreed that a young child needs a strong, reciprocal attachment with loving adults. If *too* many adults are in his life, as in a large day-care center with much turnover, he will not have a steady, dependable presence to count on. This can inhibit a child from forming trusting relationships later on in life. So people involved in day care today try hard to see that noninstitutionalized, personal care by constant, unchanging figures is given to every child.

Actually, a study into children's maternal attachment showed children who were left in good day-care facilities no less attached to their mothers than were children who remained at home in their mother's full-time care. But the day-care children had the extra dividend of being better able to form other strong attachments. They were considerably better at interacting with other people besides their parents than were the children who stayed at home.

Older children in day care need the opportunity to experiment with their own competency. A danger of a day-care center is that, like other institutions, it may sacrifice the needs of the individual for institutional efficiency. A childish spirit may be squelched in a teacher's desire for order. It is important for a single parent to keep in mind that these early years are when a child learns the concepts of his life. He is always observing behaviors and value systems that he puts together into one of his own. To drop a child in a day-care situation that offers disjointed or dissonant attitudes from your own is not a good idea. He is there far too many hours a day not to absorb its life.

Yet group care with careful concern by parent and staff can be beneficial to a child. Most authorities believe that the opportunity to learn cooperation and diversity can have real value for a child of these complicated times. Also, some of the inherent loneliness in being the child of a single parent can be greatly alleviated by positive day-care experiences; in fact, a parent who can choose between at-home baby-sitting and out-of-the-home day care should weigh the decision on several counts. The quality of the caretaking person, the availability of other children in the at-home situation, the opportunities for real skill learning in the group situation are often as important as the security gained from staying at home in a one-to-one surrogate parent arrangement.

There are actually many avenues of child care for the single parent to explore. One person chooses full-time motherhood, courtesy of welfare; one man high-priced, full-time housekeepers paid for by a high executive salary. In between these parenting roles are a variety of other choices in how to best care for a child at various stages of his life. They are choices that require thoughtful consideration. Ideally, a good deal of the consideration should take place before the decision to be a single parent is made.

The Social Realities of Being a Single Parent

"I USED TO THINK I knew what being lonely was," Elizabeth said. "If my parents went out and left me alone, I'd carry on when they came back about how lonely I'd been by myself. God!" she cried passionately, "what I'd give for a little privacy like that now! I'll tell you what lonely is. Being in an apartment day after day with a two-year-old, where nobody gives a damn how you're making out, and you don't have the freedom to even take a walk by yourself."

Then there's Rebecca, who is also a single mother.

"Lonely? Are you joking? For the first time in my life, I feel I'm not alone. There's always someone here for me to love and who loves me. And it's a deeper feeling than any relationship I've ever had in my life. It's brought more dimensions to living than I ever dreamed possible."

Obviously these two girls stand at opposite ends of the single parent spectrum. Along the line that separates them will be varying degrees of response to the reality of having sole responsibility for a child. Because single parents are individual people, and not an easily categorized group, their separate life situations affect this response. If a person is gregarious and needs other people for companionship, then the isolating aspects of being a single parent can be grim. There can be rather desperate feelings of social deprivation, as in Elizabeth's case, where money is tight. The world is out there and you cannot take part in it unless you take the baby along with you or find someone competent to leave him home with. While both solutions to loneliness are possible, life certainly is not as carefree as having no one to be responsible to but yourself.

"How I miss just the spontaneity of things," Elizabeth says. "The idea that you can accept a spur-of-the-moment invitation, or decide to go to a movie because you see there's one playing you like. With a child, everything is such a production!"

Elizabeth's sense of deprivation over being a single parent is somewhat more extreme than many other parents involved in this book. For a variety of reasons, her love for her child is not able to compensate for the problems parenthood has imposed on her. But nearly every single parent at some point early in her life as a parent, confronted the changes that had come from having a child.

Even with people who relish independence and privacy, there is a relationship between their feelings about parenthood and the amount of other people in their lives. Rebecca, for example, loves the idea that "at some point everyone goes home, and I can close the door and just be with my baby." But she readily admits that because a great number of people do walk through her door, her life is particularly happy. Rebecca is fortunate in having a number of friends who have followed through on their early enthusiasm for her decision to be a single mother. They promised to help her with baby-sitting, and they have kept their promise. Rarely is there no one available if she needs to leave her daughter for a while. Of course, Rebecca is an incredibly warm, easygoing person, and there is no doubt that the response she gives to people influences their own reactions to her. Only Ebenezer Scrooge could probably hold back from being touched by Rebecca's joyous zest for life, which includes her motherhood.

Sheila, on the other hand, like Elizabeth finds that friends have dwindled since she became a mother.

"It's not that they're not around," she says pensively. "I mean in an emergency, I could call on any one of a number of people. But I feel I'm imposing on them if I bring the baby along places that they invite me. No one I know has a child, and let's face it, what do they need an eighteen-month-old kid along for when they're partying. No one's ever told me not to bring her, but no one's talked me *into* bringing her either, when I say I can't come because I don't have a sitter."

Sheila's pride is involved in her staying home while her friends play. The same is true for Elizabeth. Particularly because they are people who have chosen to take untraveled cultural paths, they dislike having to admit the paths may be more than they can handle.

"I complain a lot," says Elizabeth, "but I'd never beg for help." Of course, it is hard to know how much Elizabeth's or Sheila's "complaints" in a negative way also influence their friends' responses. While no one may want a small child along, they may want even less a person who is disgruntled and self-pitying. In the sometimes vicious circle of human interaction, a single parent who is sensitive about her role may read her friends' behavior incorrectly. In turn, her defensiveness puts them off, and a self-fulfilling prophecy of diminishing friendship begins to take place.

One of the major reasons single parents often seek some kind of communal living arrangement is to have companionship that contains more mutuality than Sheila and Elizabeth feel they have in their friendships now. Ginger, who lives in an urban commune, has no compunction about leaving her daughter while she goes off to a museum. For one thing, she knows her daughter will be comfortably "at home" while home without her. And for another, she knows she will supervise some other children in the commune while their parents are away.

"It's marvelous not to have to feel beholden," she says, and then talked about how really difficult she had found living alone before she moved to the commune.

"And I'm a private person," she says. "But you don't know how cut off you can feel as a single parent, particularly in a city. No matter how independent you are, how capable, you have no idea how difficult life is without any help." Ginger moved to the commune when her daughter was a toddler, the age that Elizabeth's child is now. It was an age that brought Ginger's living problems to a head. Like many single mothers, she had spent the first year of her baby's life in relative solitude. For many girls, after the first euphoric feeling of accomplishment, there is a time of taking stock, of settling into the new role. While they kept up their few good friendships, many sought no really active social life. Again, the reasons for this varied. Some felt no need to, others felt uncertain how to make the adjustments motherhood entailed. Discontent, however, did not really close in until several months had gone by. By the time a child approaches his second year, the novelty of motherhood has worn off, and the child himself begins to make his presence much more actively known.

"I used to take my daughter to art galleries all the time when she was a baby," Ginger said. "I'd keep her in a back sling and pop a pacifier in her mouth and I could take my time, even do some sketching. But when she started to walk, she had to go in a stroller. I'll never forget," she said, "I think it was what really decided me that I couldn't go on living by myself. There was a great exhibit at the modern art museum. One I'd been panting to see since I heard it was coming. So I planned for weeks to go on the first sunny day. I packed up my daughter and the stroller and went off. And let me tell you, dragging a stroller and a child down three flights of apartment stairs, and then doing the same thing on a subway . . . you can't imagine how exhausting it is. And confusing! Do you push her in the subway or collapse the stroller and carry it? And what if she decides she doesn't want to walk, or starts pulling away from you on the platform? God—just getting through the subway doors is a monumental strategy session. I missed three trains before I managed to do it. I guess you get more agile with practice, but in the beginning it's impossible."

Finally, she recalled, they got to the museum station and went through similar routines coming out of the train and up the subway stairs. Ginger's tension probably accounted for her daughter's sudden crying attack, which took place as soon as they reached the street.

"I don't know," Ginger says, "she may just have been shocked by the sunlight after the subway darkness, but in the middle of the street she shrieked and carried on and wouldn't sit in the damn stroller. It was really a nightmare!"

So they stopped for cookies and milk, "which they charged me a dollar for," and at last arrived at the museum. "I wanted to cry, much louder than my daughter did," Ginger recalled. "I was just so exhausted. I had been looking forward to it so, and now I was here and all I could think of was how was I going to make that whole horrible trip back? But anyway, I paid my admission and started to push the stroller through the turnstile, when this guard stopped me and told me strollers weren't allowed. I picked up the baby in one swoop, and threw her in the man's arms and said, 'You take care of her then. I'm going to see that exhibit if it kills me!' "

Fortunately the man was sympathetic, and did in fact, watch the baby long enough for Ginger to take a fast look at what she would have liked several hours to savor. On the way home in a cab, which she could only afford because she knew the alternate price was her sanity, she decided independent parenting in a large city needs some support to make it possible.

While concrete support is not always available, single parents say that after the first shock most old friends do at least show emotional support for their decision to keep or adopt a child.

"It takes them a while to feel comfortable about it," says Steve. "My friends used to trek up here to New Hampshire after I adopted Billy and moved away, and I know it was curiosity that brought them. But after they saw it working, they really were obviously impressed. More than they should have been in my opinion. I'm not doing anything so special, really." Steve's modesty is genuine, but so is his friends' admiration. It is hard for them to really be articulate about just why they feel so warmly toward him. One man said, "I don't know, it's kind of how I feel about another friend of mine who's become terribly successful in the theater. It's nice to know someone who's made good. I feel that way about Steve. He's made good on really very special levels. He's done his own thing and done it successfully, while most of us sheep just plod along the same old way. In a way, of course, I envy him, but I know my own limitations enough to know I couldn't do what he's doing, and that helps me admit how much I admire that he can."

Ilse says that even now, after her daughter is in day care and not part of the university English department where she spent her first year of life, her coworkers frequently let her know of their admiration. A girl who is on a competitive level with Ilse and who had never been particularly warm toward her asked recently whether she "had ever really told you how much I respect you?"

Coming from her, Ilse said, that was an enormous compliment, more than any similar compliment from a close friend. "It made me feel so warm," Ilse said. "I had made contact with someone I never dreamed I'd be able to. It's as if through the baby I had transcended the unpleasanter parts of human contact—you know, competing, jealousy—I went around smiling all day."

It is odd as you explore this revolutionary life-style that you find so many stories guaranteed to create smiles of old-fashioned sentiment. One anecdote that Jo Ann tells concerns an older man she had worked with who had advised her to give the baby up for adoption because he felt it would be best for them both. "I always had a great deal of respect for him," Jo Ann said, "and I worried that he'd disapprove of me, first when he found out I was pregnant, and then when I decided to keep the baby. But he came to see me in the hospital, and brought me roses and was just marvelous. And then," she remembered, "he got up and closed the door, and like some character in an English novel, asked if he could marry me to give the baby a name."

There had been nothing romantic in their relationship. He was a widower old enough to be Jo Ann's father. In fact, he was, she knew, contemplating marriage with a lovely older woman.

"I realized that he was just genuinely concerned about this child whom he had no responsibility for in any possible way. But he never had any children of his own, and he said he felt that he'd like a new baby to have every possible chance."

" 'What's wrong with giving him my name? Why is yours so much better?' " she asked him. "I pretended to be angry," Jo Ann recalled, "but of course I wasn't and we just talked about it for a while, and I convinced him I felt capable of handling my situation on my own. And he had to admit that for a man of sixty to take on a first child might be a bit much!"

On her son's first birthday, her friend sent a huge parcel of toys with a card that said, "Take pride today in being your mother's son."

"A few weeks later," Jo Ann said, "he got married. I just know he held off to see how I'd make out."

Kleenex anyone?

Most adoptive mothers found their new status generally accepted by old friends. When the child was interracial, a few did sniff in disapproval and disappear. "But that's their problem," Betty said. "My only regret is that it took me so long to find out what kind of people they were." Some of their other friendships also went through changes when they became parents. As older unmarried women, they had many friends in similar circumstances. When Betty's and Jean's own circumstances changed, a couple of these women found it difficult to maintain their earlier relationships. Both Betty and Jean feel their friends were largely troubled by envy, and psychologists I talked to agreed with their assessment.

"Particularly," one man explained, "if they feel incapable of the other women's courage, they will resent them." Jean also says that these friendships involved sharing external rather than internal experiences.

"We weren't really intimate as people," she says. "So when I was suddenly unavailable to go to the theater, or play bridge, we found we had nothing to talk about."

Betty agrees with this, but feels that it works both ways. "I wasn't interested in them either," she says. "Through my daughter, I met other people with children, and I found myself becoming friendly with them, at least on certain superficial levels. But mainly, aside from my really close friends, I wanted to spend as much free time as I could alone with Kathi. That put my old friends off, too. Without children of their own, they couldn't really understand that. And having them over wasn't successful because they just about acted as if Kathi weren't there . . . expecting me to act the same. So, we just drifted apart." It is a drift that obviously causes her little concern.

While Betty and Jean were discussing unmarried friends, single mothers occasionally find that married friends will develop resentment in place of their old affection. Particularly if they themselves find married motherhood trying, they may resent a single mother's assumption that she can manage the role on her own. And often the "friends' " resentment increases as the single mother's success becomes more apparent.

Marion says that when she first had her daughter, she would occasionally tell an old friend who lived in the same building about some of her adjustment problems. "But after a while, I couldn't take the glee I saw in her eyes. That 'I told you so' message was loud and clear even though she didn't say it directly. Actually, she *had* advised me not to have the baby, but once I did I thought she'd be sympathetic. Of course, she hates staying home with her kids and her husband won't let her get a job, so I guess I can understand her feelings."

New people who enter the single parent's life seem generally able to adjust to the idea that they are dealing with a single person who is also a parent. "I tell them right away, though," says Ilse. "I don't want anyone, men in particular, to think I'm unencumbered, and I don't like any speculation about my marital status."

Some men, and occasionally one of the women friends of the single fathers, will be put off by the news that the person they find so attractive shares their charm with a child. But this attitude usually reflects not so much disapproval, as simply no desire to get involved in what would now be a more complicated relationship. The issue of how to manage a social life, however, even with people who accept their particular problems, is itself a sticky one for many single parents. If they are often reluctant to discipline their children because they have been separated all day by work, they are even more concerned about leaving their children at the end of the day to go out on dates.

"I feel terribly torn about it," Edith says. "Here I am getting all dressed up, leaving him alone again after he's been without me so much already. He always cries when I leave," she said, sighing. "Always. It's not exactly the music to go out dancing by."

Of course, children with two parents also cry when their parents go out. The simple truth is that the egocentricity of a small child dominates his view of relationships, particularly with his parents. There is never enough contact to please him. But this does not obscure another truth, which is that too much contact can smother him and bring its own serious problems.

"What the single parent is doing," one psychiatrist said, "is taking away the sanction of tradition. Thousands of people leave their children quite excessively, but the fact that they're married and maintaining a culturally legitimate social life allows them to rationalize it." He agreed that the single parent does, however, have an extra burden by being the one parent the child has to relate to, and consequently feel deprived of.

"Certainly I would advise them not to leave the child every other night on a continuous basis. Look," he said, "they really have to play it by ear. Certain periods of the child's life will be easier, and certain situations will make it easier." He explained that if, for example, the child has something pleasurable to do, like visit a grandmother, or stay overnight with a close friend, his mother's going out will be relatively simple. As a child gets older and has more independent interests, it's also easier. "Not always, though," the doctor added, "because then other kinds of problems enter the scene, like the child's attitudes toward the parent dating, and the dates themselves."

Gary, as the quintessentially eligible bachelor, has a long line of girls waiting to play mommy on a Sunday afternoon outing with his son.

"For a while I was doing that scene," Gary said. "I thought it would be nice for Mike to have a woman around, so we'd go off somewhere with one of my girl friends and then give him an early supper while we had a snack. Then after he was settled, we'd clean up and go out to a movie or a late supper. Ideal, right?" he asked me, smiling. But then, Gary said, the counselor that he had continued to see with his son, pointed out that perhaps he was giving Mike an image of rather random commitments to relationships. This was particularly troublesome as the girls in their zeal for real commitments from Gary often overwhelmed Mike with affection on the days they were with him.

"I hadn't realized it from his end," Gary says ruefully. "I deliberately didn't stick with one person because I didn't want them to imply anything about the relationship that wasn't there. But as far as Mike was concerned, it was really traumatic. He'd get to like someone over two or three times, and then zap, they'd be gone for two months. He'd ask me about them and I'd flash the big smile and pull out the new lady of the day. It was really idiotic of me. Now, it's Mike and me and an occasional friend. There are two or three girls who are on my wave length about marriage, and when one of them can join me they do. I'll conduct my romances off Mike's time from now on."

Many single parents, male and female, try for some kind of separation between their adult social lives and their lives as parents. Like Gary, they are concerned that a procession of people in a child's life can be confusing. While this is true, keeping the child totally separate from the parent's social life is not the best solution, either. It creates an aura of mystery about the parent, and there are enough mysteries already about the world and growing up for a child to deal with. It may also interfere with Oedipal adjustments. Parents should never be seductive with their children, but neither should they ever deny their own adult male or femaleness. A child would undoubtedly be discomfitted by seeing his mother in too obviously sexual a light with some male friend. But this does not mean that he should be denied seeing her interact as a woman with a man. And if he never gets the opportunity to meet his mother's friends (or his father's), he may begin to feel there is something "wrong" with the friends, and even ultimately with anyone of that sex.

Furthermore, should the parent ever become serious about one particular person, the child will not have had the chance to gradually develop his own, hopefully positive, attitudes toward that person. Several parents had the idea that it was better to wait until they really liked someone before bringing that person home. But they should remember that the level of their involvement will be far ahead of their children's when this happens. One formerly single mother has great regrets over how she handled the relationship with the man she eventually married. Their problems now, and there are quite a few, she feels stem from her son's resentment over the sudden appearance in his life of a man destined to be his father.

"I thought he would naturally feel the way I did, but of course that was ridiculous," she said. "And probably the fact that I was so obviously in love accentuated his tentativeness." On the other hand, the man she was in love with was impatient to marry, once they had decided marriage was what they wanted. He was not prepared to wait indefinitely for his future stepson to decide it was all right to enter his life. Had she brought her husband into her single home earlier, Sylvia is sure the problems she is having now in her new home would be far less severe.

Some children may feel their parents resent them for interfering with their adult good times. Because research does show that children of single parents worry about separation, making a child feel that he is in the way will make that child's sense of security shaky. This is why the arrangement of taking a child along to parties or ski weekends begins to be less satisfactory sometimes, as the child gets older. Unless he is really old enough to keep himself busy with his own interests, he can feel that his presence is not entirely delightful to his mother or father. Probably he is right, and a parent who wants to take her child along rather than stay home or leave him home, should realize that he is sensitive to her response at having him around. The truth is that he *will* make her experience less carefree, but she really has no right to be angry with him for that particular reason.

Marion stopped taking her daughter to ski weekends when the one couple with children dropped out of the ski club. "The first weekend I went as the only one with a child, it was really terrible," she says. "I was self-conscious and then I left her with someone from the hotel staff who wasn't at all eager for the job. Knowing that, I didn't really enjoy the skiing, so of course I was rotten and inside I blamed it on my daughter. I came back to the lodge, and she was crying, and I yelled at her way out of proportion. I felt guilty, of course, so I took her upstairs and cuddled her until she fell asleep. But then," she says, and her cheeks flush with guilt, "I went downstairs, and we had cocktails and started to dance and I lost track of the time. Finally someone—not me," she says grimly, "heard her screaming. I went up and the poor kid was soaking wet and so scared. And for days afterward she kept coming over to me and asking for a kiss, and I know she felt I was angry at her, even though she didn't really understand why. I felt incredibly guilty and I'll never do it again. It was my decision to be a mother, and if I can't always act like an irresponsible teen-ager, I can't make *her* feel guilty about it."

How to handle sexual relationships is an obvious issue in the life of a single parent. Whether or not this becomes a problem depends on the parent's own attitudes. Many single mothers who have abandoned old ideas of sexual morality feel comfortable about having men occasionally stay overnight in their apartments, or even live with them for extended periods of time. Of the single fathers I talked to, none said they had women spend the night under the roof they shared with their sons. They may only have been concerned with maintaining the adoption agency's approval, but the fact remains that except for those who lived in a commune, sex and fatherhood were kept separate. In a commune, of course, the situation is different. In a Maine commune, sexual relationships between commune members are open and accepted. No attempt is made to keep this fact from the children, although again, sexual display is not flaunted. Because the commune members do not believe in monogamy, and do believe that sexual expression is part of a relationship, they are unabashed about having their children share these attitudes.

"I don't mean that they watch us making love," Victor, one of the communal fathers, said. "But they do come in and see us in bed, and often without clothes on. I can't pretend that their values about sex are the same as a child from a middle-class home. Obviously, I expect that they'll grow up with similar attitudes to ours, and maybe have their own sexual experiences earlier than other children, although I'm not so sure of that. But in any case, I think they'll be healthier people sexually."

It is hard to argue with him when statistics show that many children from the most traditional homes are in fact having intercourse earlier and earlier, many losing their virginity in the junior high school years. Few children in the commune begin experiencing sex any earlier than that. The difference lies in the sanction.

In the commune, and in many single parents' noncommunal homes, there is in fact some attempt made to balance "progressive" attitudes toward sexual expression with an understanding of what a child is emotionally ready to handle. The traditional psychological idea that a child can be overly stimulated by sexual display, and emotionally troubled by experiences he is not sufficiently mature to understand, is not being totally abandoned. The majority of single mothers do not openly engage in provocative kinds of behavior in their own homes. It is the rare single mother who would have more than one man in her child's life at a time. She might be sleeping with several men, but she would never make the child aware of how interchangeable her bed partners were. Again, the single mother's reasons have less to do with morality than with not wanting the child to feel his mother is casual about love relationships—a judgment that might be applied to the mother's feeling for him.

"I'd have no apology about living with someone for a while who was nice to the baby," Rebecca says. "And then having him move out and some time later having someone else here. But they would be reasonably steady relationships, not one-night stands. As long as *I'm* here steadily, I don't see what harm would come from Emily having other people in her life for a while who related to her. If it were women roommates, no one would make a fuss. Why should the fact that I sleep with the person threaten her, if I'm discreet, which obviously I would be? Her sense of security is going to come from how well I exercise my responsibility to her. As long as I do that, my adult relationships, no matter what they are, shouldn't make her less secure."

How these viewpoints register in our own cultural cameras depends on how able we are to separate ourselves from the fixed pictures of our conditioning. The assumption that a child's adjustment to the world would be damaged by witnessing anything but a monogamous relationship is certainly being questioned, since monogamous marriage is open to much harsher evaluation than it ever has been before.

Some single parents, of course, are quite conventional in their attitudes about sexual display. Unless they marry, no man will become a permanent part of their households. And marriage is something that many single parents do think about. They may, like Ilse, see it as a practical move for the future. "I'd like to marry someone with enough money so I wouldn't have to work forever," she says. "But I'd have to really like him a lot, and he'd have to really like the baby. And we'd have to allow each other enough freedom to be ourselves. Either that," she says with a grin, "or I'd want to be madly in love!"

Edith has always pictured herself married, and still believes that she may find someone to place in that picture. Her decision to have her baby was simply that pregnancy came before "he" came along. Still, the longer they remain unmarried, the more concern single parents have about how marriage would affect their relationships with their children.

However, the more certain single parents are about their lifestyles, the more likely they are to make the kind of marriage that will work for themselves and their children. If marriage is perceived as a relationship between equals, then the single parent, strong in her identities as person and parent, can best deal with the difficulties adding a second parent to a family often entails.

For an unmarried parent may find herself in the middle of conflict between her new husband and her child. The same, of course, holds true for the single father who marries. Despite all of today's psychological awareness and transitional flexibility, a child may still resent a new love figure in his parent's life; and an adult may resent the child's prior and insistent demands on the new wife or husband. Resulting frustrations can be great. The single parent who marries should realize that it will take time for everyone to feel comfortable with one another. But they do seem to have an advantage over many widowed or divorced parents who remarry. For children of single parents are usually open to an extended idea of family. If a parent is careful not to make the child feel pushed out of place by the new person who has moved in, the child should be able to believe his mother or father can love someone else and still love him, too.

A reason, in fact, that many single parents consider marriage has more to do with their children's welfare than with their own.

"I don't want my daughter to ever have to feel responsible for me," Annette says. "I can see as she gets older where it would be nice for her to feel she didn't have to worry about my needing companionship. Not that I expect I ever will, but a child may perceive her role in a household like this as particularly responsible. Anyway," she finished, "it's something I think about."

That they do think about it is, of course, the best indication that a person can manage balancing the social needs of a single person with the demands of being a growing child's single parent.

The Alternative Life-Style

"Remember that Simon and Garfunkel folk song a few years ago?" Jerry, a member of a Maine commune, asked. "You know, the one that speaks about the 'sounds of silence . . . people talking without speaking, people hearing without listening . . . No one dared disturb the sounds of silence.' Well," he said, "we're trying our damndest to disturb that soulless silence we all came out of. Here, we do listen, and we do speak. . . . We're learning," he finished predictably, "to be together."

That lace-edged, heavily merchandized idea of family called "togetherness"—are there any traces of its choking sweetness pressed between the pages of our new vocabulary books? The contemporary definition of togetherness makes it easier to understand what at first might seem contradictory about the single parent and communal living. Even as they eagerly speculate on the extended family, they almost religiously revere ideas of autonomy and independence. The paradox disintegrates with a little speculation, for it is not just they who they insist be independent; nearly every single parent is conscious of wanting to instill a strong sense of independence in his child.

This desire to encourage deep feelings of identity in children means of course unlocking them from the dependencies of the nuclear family. If there were some single parents who used this as a rationale for not assuming their own responsibilities, others (if you will, those who are most "together") really seemed to be motivated out of the children's best interests. Betty, for example, says that as a single parent, and particularly as an older parent, "I want Kathi to be secure in herself, and open to other relationships so that she doesn't need me too much. I worry that something will happen to me before she grows up and I try to give her as many tools as possible so she'll be able to cope. I'm convinced," she adds, "that the best way for her to get those tools is to be exposed to all different kinds of people, and to learn not to be afraid to reach out and take them into her life."

And then she spoke of her own family, and how she had always felt rejected by her brothers, and although she wouldn't admit it until many years later, by her mother. "We were all so competitive for my mother's affection that we could never get close to each other. I think in a terrible way my mother manipulated us to compete for her like that. Maybe it eased her own feeling of rejection by my father." She looked up then and laughed. "It all sounds terribly sick, but I assure you we were the typical American family. It was only when I was in analysis that I realized how sick that kind of family can be! Well, Kathi may not have a father, and no brothers or sisters, but I guarantee you she'll have deeper feelings toward other people than I ever was able to have."

Jean put a huge mirror in her daughter's room, with a measuring stick alongside it. She has her daughter measure herself once a month and makes a chart and much ado about how the child is growing into a "big girl."

"I stress not the inches that she's growing, but that she's maturing. I want her to have a real sense of herself as a separate person. And the more people that can reflect my daughter back to herself, the more dimensions, it seems to me, her sense of self will have."

It is understandable that single parents who had the independence to assume a role historically couched in dependency, would see independence as a characteristic they want to cultivate in their own children. And because they recognize that parenthood was their personal choice, and not a role imposed on them by society, they can de-mystify the parent-child relationship. Most single parents see being a parent as only one of the ways they experience themselves as people. This vision allows them to see their children as separate people who do not have to reinforce the parents' identities by total and exclusive dependence.

With this philosophy, both Betty and Jean see value in the communal life-style. Betty is already making plans to jointly purchase some land in the country with several friends where she can commute part-time to teach. On the days she is away, other members of the group will care for Kathi, as Betty will do for their children when it is her turn to be home. They plan to rotate individual work schedules so that this group schedule becomes possible.

Jean already has an extended family relationship with the friends who care for her daughter during the week. At the end of the day, when Jean comes by to pick her up, the little girl will sometimes cling to her mother substitute rather than run out to greet her "real" mother. Jean says, and seems to mean it, that she is not resentful or threatened when this happens.

"Look," she says, "I want her to love my friend. I couldn't leave her with someone she *didn't* care about. And after all, I want to go to work instead of staying home all the time. So she doesn't want to *come* home every time. It's perfectly natural. Besides, the more love relationships she has in her life, the better job I'll feel I've done as her parent."

Many other single parents are attracted to some aspect of the communal life. Some of their reasons are pragmatic. For one thing, it is a more accepting environment for what they are trying to do. Judy, a single mother in her mid-twenties, brought her baby back to the highly ethnic neighborhood in which she herself was raised. Her reason was that the rents reflected those earlier days, but unfortunately so did the attitudes of her neighbors. She feels she's the community's "scarlet woman," which at first was amusing, but now seems much less so. "It gets to you after awhile," she says. "First of all they're always spying on me. No, really," she adds, obviously not wanting to seem paranoic. "It's true. Anyone who's black or has long hair or wears 'funny clothes' is automatically assumed to be heading for my house. And if I do have any visitors, there's always someone wandering around the hall on some pretext. They're nice enough to the baby, but when he gets older, he's going to realize what they think of me. I've got to get out before that. I'm not going to have him feel those kinds of judgments, particularly when I have no apology to make about his status!"

The commune also offers concrete help in meeting the many reality demands of single parenthood. Judy longs for a friendly neighbor to drop the baby off with sometimes, or one on whom she can call for grocery shopping if the baby is asleep or too sick to take outside. "They're little things," she says, "but they build up. You can feel so really alone if there's no one around to count on for *any* help. That's why a commune seems so great to me. Imagine—whole bunches of people to share with, to relate to. It must be terrific!"

Yet Judy's excitement about the possibilities of communal living suggests something greater than pragmatism. Her talk of sharing and relating is heard from many single parents attracted to the extended family life-style. They seem in a figurative sense really like immigrants, leaving old boundaries of family behind, for the open land of wider concepts of family relationships. They look to the commune as the natural environment to form these relationships, to develop, with their children, intimacy and trust with a number of people.

This thread, unraveling old ideas of exclusivity, seems truly to tie many single parents together. So many, both men and women, are really trying to push open the doors of family to let in other people. To yank the definition of family out of the laboratory where blood ties tell you who to love. To abandon possessiveness and long-term promises extracted in claustrophobic love-grasps. To instead relate as one whole person to another whole person, child or adult, with whom you share intensely certain days of your life, free of the fear that other people may take your place some other time.

These then are the goals, and the thinking that lead many single parents to seek out some form of communal living. How successful a family life-style it is for single parents depends on what kind of communes they attempt to create or become a part of. If anything is certain about these times we live in, it is that our future will hold a great many varieties of family arrangements, many of which will have some communal base. But right now, we are witnessing an enormous range of experimentation. The single parent who is speculating about communal living should be reasonably aware of some of the problems built into the search for Utopia, particularly when the search is in its early stages. The labels *commune* and *extended family* are actually umbrella terms. When an adoption agency asks a single parent to provide some evidence of an extended family, it rarely means more than the availability of close friends or relatives who can take over if the parent needs help. (And, as indicated, someone of the opposite sex for the child to identify with as a role model.) Then there are extended family arrangements where the families live separately but "in community" as Steve, one of the single fathers, did in New Hampshire. There are other communal setups, urban and rural, where families live together under one roof, sharing all aspects of family life.

In some communes individual members will hold jobs in the outside community, while in others work as well as family life will be confined to the commune itself. Sometimes, however, the work of the commune is offered for sale. The products can range from candles or leather goods sold at roadside stands to the highly successful Bruderhof community that manufactures toys and children's furniture under the name of Community

Playthings.

The Bruderhofs are really an exception, for economics are often a problem for communes, with many commune members relying on welfare checks to keep themselves and their "family" going. The desire to remain outside the jungle of the marketplace makes it difficult to reach the philosophical goal of counter-cultural self-sufficiency.

Some communes where the residents pursue outside careers, will soften their moral dilemma by operating as an economic collective. The collective aspect may, in rural communities, consist simply of farming a jointly owned piece of land. But in city or country, it may also mean sharing all possessions, and even all the salaries earned by individual members. Many such collectives were initially created out of a desire to try to restructure people's financial ties to society. One commune, for example, was begun by a group of people involved in helping draft resisters get over the border to Canada. They were all working together but living separately. Eventually it occurred to them that they were paying a great deal of money for duplication of services. As a group, their rent, transportation, food, and other costs could be greatly curtailed. Similarly, many single parents who are attracted to urban communes also found the idea originating from an economic base. With city life as expensive as it is, why not join with a group under one roof and share expenses?

The emotional life-styles of communes can vary widely. Some communities are psychologically oriented, with a dominant goal of self-actualization. The members may regularly engage in sensitivity sessions, with great emphasis placed on developing self-awareness and improving relationships with other people. There are several political groups who consider themselves revolutionaries, who want to work at their anarchistic goals in a more unified way. There are religious movements such as Yoga Asram or the well-known Jesus Freaks. And there are some effective self-help communities, perhaps the best known being Synanon or Camp Hill Village. One girl who suffered from a serious drug problem went to a commune aimed at taking people off drugs. Pregnant when she arrived, she had her baby while part of the program and continues to live there, off drugs, raising her child and working toward helping other new members experience what she considers to be the "best trip of her life."

Communes will vary in size from a handful of people to over two hundred in Bruderhof Village. Some communes are open to anyone who cares to join, others restrict membership to certain numbers and certain types of people. Actually, there is a kind of self-selection that usually operates at a commune, with the people who are not suited to its life, for whatever reason, deciding on their own to leave. This is fortunate, because there is great reluctance among most people engaged in communal living to exercise the kind of "heavy" authority that asking someone to leave implies.

And many people do leave communes, just as many communes fail soon after their creation. The testing of beliefs, the actual experiencing of abstract ideas is not without pitfalls. The communal movement is not new in this country; it goes back well over a hundred years. There are, of course, many differences between those earlier communes and the ones we see today, but there is one problem both share and that should be noted by the single parent. Throughout the communal movement the relationship of children to parents has presented problems that threaten the communes' cohesion. In contemporary communes, a great deal of adult dissension and children's confusion results from discrepant attitudes toward parent-child relationships.

In most communes, there is always some concept that the children belong to the extended family. The degree of this possession, however, can be a major source of conflict. To what degree does the child "belong" to the natural parent, and to what degree to the larger community? Should a parent go out of his way to treat his child as he would any other child in the group, playing down any suggestion of special treatment or possessiveness? There are many psychologists who will tell you such parental objectivity is not really possible, although other experiments in communal living do not always bear this out. A parent does not necessarily have to care less about his child in order not to play favorites, or to allow other adults to share significantly in the child's life. The kibbutz of Israel seems to be a good example of this model. The child is exposed to several "mothering" figures, as well as several father figures. He learns to love many people besides his parents but retains an ongoing awareness of his parents' identities. It is important to remember, however, that in a kibbutz the adults are in agreement about the system of child care. In our contemporary communes, so many of which are in the embryonic stages, attitudes are not always so unified.

Single parents, therefore, despite their sincerity about wanting to free their children from the nuclear family model, may find the actual experience of commune-as-family difficult to deal with. We are after all products of our own socialization. Merely rejecting the past does not, unfortunately, always keep us from acting out of its conditioning. The actual surrendering of parental autonomy to a group structure may be impossible for some parents.

In the Maine commune, forty-four adults live together in what was once an old inn. There are also twenty-two children who sleep in a large ballroom converted to a dormitory. Seven members of the commune, five women and two men, take care of the children. The majority of the other members work, at least intermittently, at outside jobs. While there is no barrier to an individual parent's spending time with her own child, the children do live together as a group and seem to relate to all adult members as parent surrogates. And, in those instances where the commune feels a decision should be made about a particular child, the group's decision takes precedence over the parent's potentially opposing view.

Lauren, who moved there with her son Ricky when he was two years old, for a long while turned off comments by other members about the boy's lack of speech. "I just couldn't deal with them telling me what to do. I felt intruded on. It was ridiculous. After all, I wanted to live in a collective. No one forced me to live that way. But I couldn't handle it. And I felt really guilty, because I knew for Ricky's sake I ought to check him out. But you know," she said then, "the real truth is I didn't want to find out he was brain damaged or something, because I had tried to abort him on my own when I was pregnant. I've always felt I probably damaged him. I was being cowardly and childish, not wanting to know. If I hadn't lived with the group, God knows how long I would have kept my head in the sand."

At a group meeting, the commune officially overruled her and Ricky was taken for extensive neurological tests at the commune's expense. He was diagnosed as having a hearing problem that was corrected later that year, and paid for once more by the community's medical fund.

This particular commune is fairly tightly run, and it is doubtful that Lauren could have persisted in her attitude and remained a welcome member. They do all try to maintain group solidarity around certain principles, many of which have to do with the child's relationship to the extended family. The "family" in this sense includes other children as well as other adults. There is a fairly commonly held belief among most communal people that peer-group relationships are a major aspect of a child's development. Many professional people agree with this point of view. One of the major arguments against the nuclear family is that it precludes opportunity for really strong peer-group identification.

Children who live in apartment houses or suburban homes have little really intimate contact with other children. Their visits are planned and sporadic, with mothers making "arrangements" rather than the play evolving spontaneously just from being together. Studies of children who have had really good group relationships with other children show they grow into people who are extremely resilient, flexible, and sensitive to others' needs.

A dramatic example of this socialization is seen in an article by Anna Freud where she describes five young children who had lost their parents in infancy while all were imprisoned in a concentration camp. For the duration of the war, these children took care of each other inside the camp, and she vividly describes them as being, even at the age of three, quite beautifully mature in their social and emotional relationships.

A boy in the Vermont commune whose mother had gone to England to study and had taken him with her was so unhappy away from his friends that he asked to be returned on his own. Although he misses his mother, the choice remains his to stay on without her. He is, by the way, described by other members of the commune as a child particularly able to relate to other people, old or young, within their private commune world and in the larger one outside.

One of the frequent criticisms of the communal way of life is that it does not really prepare its children for "real life." This, of course, is a sentiment commune members do not share. For one thing they question what "real life" is, or at least what it is going to be by the time their children grow up. As one man said, "My guess is that they will inherit a situation where not just a few 'freaks' like us, but a great number of people will simply have dropped out of the whole career, competition box. We're giving these children the tools to live in that environment so that they can hang on, even in a marginal fashion, to those aspects of society that work for them."

By tools he meant cooperation, and a different set of values. "They won't have to have every family member have a car, or feel that a TV set has to always be on just because it's there," he explains. Often out of necessity, there is also an emphasis, on mastering mechanical skills. They are actually survival skills in their broadest sense, and skills most adult males in communes regrettably lack. Because so many of these men came out of middle-class college-bound childhoods, they never learned how to be physically self-sufficient in this particular way, to live without carpenters and plumbers and electricians always on call.

"I did art history instead of learning how to use a welding rig," Bruce, a single father who lives in a southern commune with his adopted son, says. "But my son's going to be able to offer something real to his society. He's going to know how to exist independently. He'll know how to build a cabinet, and a house . . . he'll know what a water system is . . . he's going to be able to survive . . . it's we adults who have to go on welfare or work on meaningless jobs because we're too dependent on society for survival."

Many commune members really do see their children as pioneers of a new era. While they themselves pioneered into the land of communal living, they feel children of the communes will be the people truly able to rebuild society in new and exciting ways. Because of this almost evangelical worship of their possibilities, there is a great reluctance to impose a heavy adult "authority trip" on children. (And also, of course, because most commune members are so conscious of what they feel were the mistakes of their own socialization.)

The whole categorically bad, good, right, wrong-ethic many adults guiltily emerged from is left at most commune nursery doors. One psychological team that studied the child-raising methods of communes said the desire to let children really "do their own thing" extended even to the possibility that the children would move away from the communal way of life when they grew older. "Most communes," they wrote, "if faced with a choice between training the next generation of communards and training children to be free would opt for the latter."

Again, however, the principle of this may be more comfortable than the practice for some single parents. The child they raise communally will be different than the one they might have raised in a suburban community. And they may carry enough residual remnants of their own suburban upbringings to find the child uncomfortably unfamiliar. Margaret Mead has talked of how in transitional times it is to the children that adults turn for answers, as they are the only ones really able to confront the changes of the culture. This is what many commune members are suggesting in their attitudes toward child rearing. But nonetheless, an individual parent may find it occasionally threatening to her own self-concept, and to her concept of being a parent.

A random survey of children in communes finds them generally free and open people, amazingly adult in many ways, unusually childlike in others. The age and sex barriers most children are sensitive to are usually absent. They interact with almost anyone with a sense of ease. While they are not motivated to be well-mannered or responsible in a conventional sense, they seem usually to respond well to a reasonable explanation of why a particular behavior is desirable. On the other hand, they are capable of rejecting adult requests if they seem unreasonable, and to reject them loudly and, to some eyes, rudely. Certainly the possibility of making child-raising mistakes in the name of freedom is as great as the mistakes made in trying to discipline. But, at least in communes where the adult members are truly interested in the children, the children appear relatively stable in the context of their communal lives. The differences between children born in a commune and those who enter one later in life are marked. A single parent who considers moving with an older child into a communal situation should recognize that he will have a great adjustment to make. No matter how unusual their life-style seemed in a conventional community, the life-style of the commune will show that much of the traditional community's values were actually absorbed.

For adults the problems are even greater in shedding the clothes of earlier life. The girl who was the liberated spirit of a middle-class suburb may still feel painfully middle-class in some of the liberated living rooms of a commune. While not the dens of iniquity some people imagine communes to be, they generally *are* places that engage in much more casual and open sex than some people are emotionally ready for (even though they would like to be!).

However, in the at least theoretical openness of the commune such individual adjustment problems can be aired and possibly worked out. After all, the much abused "do your own thing" principle is central to attempts at communal living.

Again, this is a concept that also has a potential for conflict. The emphasis on "doing your own thing" sometimes can be poorly balanced against the other balance aimed for, that of group participation. For this reason, many people who study communes believe the crucial ingredient for success is a set of agreed-upon beliefs, and preferably also of goals. These can ease the adjustment into communal living for people who have been socialized for a different way of life. Sharing, cooperation, and compromise are part of the extended family, and these are not necessarily qualities the nuclear family teaches.

In a study of urban communes it became clear that there were two major points that determined whether the commune would be successful. One concerned the people themselves, their ability to step away from their own backgrounds, and to sublimate self-centered needs and goals for those of the groups. "The smallest things can irritate you at first," one girl said. "I never realized how I felt about messiness, for example, until I moved to the collective. I like to have my baby spotless all the time, but I used the group high chair to feed her in. The chair was always cruddy, I thought. Someone would use it before me, and never cleaned it up, at least enough to satisfy me. Finally, we had a meeting about it, and we all agreed on some principles of cleanliness that weren't really too stiff. I learned not to be so uptight, and I guess the others learned not to be quite so careless."

This principle of organized tasks and behaviors was the second requisite for a smooth-running commune as delineated in the study. People seem to need some kind of predetermined system to follow, so that doing your own thing does not result in competition or alienation.

One of the interesting dynamics of all these experiments in living is that people often move away from their own socialization with what are at first extreme behaviors. If, for example, the nuclear family was too isolated, then all aspects of isolation are automatically "bad." However, in many communal arrangements, issues such as personal privacy can be a real factor in the commune's survival. In most cases where group living is successful, some synthesis between the hunched-up privacy of earlier life and the abandonment of any idea that people do occasionally need to be by themselves is arrived at. Communes that decided all aspects of privacy were unnecessary found that relationships tended to break down. People began to behave with much more pettiness and stubbornness than in situations where some element of privacy was maintained. Many communes, therefore, do try to have people have their own bedrooms and also to have at least one room set aside for quiet personal activity. This room may be shared by other people, but the emphasis is on doing one's own, not the group's, thing.

Perhaps the most significant conclusion of studies on the commune as an alternative life-style is that there have to be really strong convictions about these alternatives for the life-style to work. The most successful communes, urban or rural, are not those where people have run to "get away," but instead, places where they have gone to try to "get it together." Single parents who consider the commune, then, should think seriously not only about what is wrong with marriage, or the nuclear family, but about how they would really rather have things be, and about how much they are willing to sacrifice to have these goals accomplished. On this note, it is interesting that many communes do well where people have come together as strangers, simply answering ads in newspapers, or hearing about each other through a mutual source. It appears that strong mutual goals can create strong bonds, so that previous friendship is not necessary if people are to live together successfully.

For the single parent who is truly committed to the idea that her child will be best prepared for life if he learns flexibility, independence, and group relating, the commune may well be an answer. She may want to begin some kind of extended family arrangement on her own, either in the country, or within the city where she now lives and works. And an extended family can assuage much of the loneliness that is sometimes part of the single parent family.

"It's great," Ginger told me, "before I moved in with the group I'd be so depressed most nights. I really couldn't afford baby-sitting except on special occasions, and I was living in a fourth-floor walk-up to save money, so not too many people visited me. When I'd put the baby to sleep, I'd have nothing but the phone and the TV set to bring another voice into my living room. Now, it's just so terrific to come downstairs after she's asleep and always know there'll be someone to talk to if I feel like talking."

Any city of any size will have some source of information about finding a commune. Health food stores, boutiques, coffee houses are usually informal information exchanges, and people are more than willing to act as liaison for interested parties. Special-interest newspapers and magazines will feature ads and will run requests by people looking for others interested in joining or creating a commune. There is at least one national commune magazine, *Alternatives Newsmagazine,* published in San Francisco, that lists existing communes, and many underground newspapers do the same. Communes already established will put interested people onto other groups in geographic areas of their choice. Nearly any college or university will have some people involved in this aspect of the counter-culture's activity who will share their information.

The problem seems much less one of how to find a commune, than to find the right commune, and most of all, to discover in oneself a real, rather than romantic, vision of what communal living promises to be.

The Psychological Effects of Having a Single Parent

CONTRARY TO OLD IDEAS that a small infant is little more than a blob of noisy moisture, research continues to prove that learning of some kind takes place almost from birth. Couple this idea with the idea fundamental to psychoanalysis, that adult emotional health relates to how emotional life was handled as a child, and you can make a single parent a nervous parent indeed.

Central to the story of the single parent are questions they and society almost inevitably ask. How will their life-style affect their children? Are there basic needs of childhood that parents are violating by choosing not to marry? And lastly, do they have the right to impose potential conflict on their children by their decision to become single parents?

"I can't imagine that the pioneer parents stopped to worry about whether they had a right to take their children across the country," Steve said to me. "They did what they felt had to be done, and they expected that their children, with their help of course, would make the best of the situation."

Many single parents share this attitude. They refuse to apologize for the possibility that their children may have some psychological problems because they are missing a parent.

"If you can find me any parent who doesn't give their child some problems, then I might feel apologetic," said Jo Ann. I can't believe that the stress for my son in not having a father is necessarily worse than the thousand other stresses he might have had instead."

That it *is* inevitable for parents to create some areas of conflict for their children is of course true. R. D. Laing came to the conclusion that in every family there is a "politics of experience." By this he means a real power struggle will take place over whose definition of reality is to be accepted. A mother who needs relief from the tediousness of child care will tell her child to go to bed early because "he's sleepy." The child of course knows he is not sleepy, or at least thinks he knows it; but this perception is thrown into conflict with his mother's need to have him out of her way. Such separate views of reality create subtle and sometimes tangible tensions. A child whose experience is regularly denied in order to meet his parents' needs can eventually become seriously confused about how valid any of his perceptions are.

Because they are aware that growing up with any set of parents has built-in hazards, few professionals will say that the children of single parents will be particularly handicapped psychologically. The idea that a child is given optimum chances for healthy development by having two people, a man and a woman, as consistent models, does still linger in most psychological thinking. However, there is new attention being paid to who the people are, and what conditions they are living in. *What* man, *what* woman, *what* child, and in what kind of cultural climate? Obviously being a single parent's child today is different from the way it would have been twenty-five years ago. And research has shown that despite nuclear family mythology, having a good relationship with one parent is healthier soil for emotional growth than growing up with two discontented parents.

"Children are often used as weapons in a marriage," a marriage counselor told me. "The husband and wife will blame each other for the child's problems, or compete with each other for his love. More often than you realize parents will manipulate their children for some very distorted needs. I can certainly see situations where one parent who was competent and stable could spare a child certain kinds of serious conflict."

To try and assess what kind of family situation is best for a child, we have to use new kinds of psychological scales. They are scales finely calibrated to pick up more and more subtle factors than any scales in the past. We cannot measure whole sets of experiences and behaviors by lumping them into one large box labeled *pathology*. Nor can we clearly define the roads to pathology. Sharp distinctions between what is "normal" and "abnormal" are suddenly blurred. It would be hard, in fact, in or out of professional circles to find agreed-upon definitions of these now almost irrelevant terms. A psychological meeting today is likely to have little resemblance to a staid gathering of mutually respected peers. The covering of civilized courtesy stretches thin as disciples of entrenched positions battle their more irreverent colleagues, who refuse to take any theory for granted, no matter how many learned generations have done so before.

It is understandable that theories about family and child development should reflect the changes in society, because the family is so fundamental *to* society. If we look back over our recent history, we can see how social influences caused such ideas to change, and what the effects of the changes in turn had on the culture. When earlier generations came here from other countries, they carried along concepts of parents as unquestioned authority figures. A child did what poppa or momma said just because they said it. He could have all kinds of inner turmoil, but if he kept it to himself and went on obeying, his parents' goals were satisfied. (This docile lockstep to parental drumbeats produced many people whose emotions were almost totally locked up).

With the birth of psychoanalysis, and with people's assimilation into the American culture, parents became concerned with their children's inner as well as outer life. They left heavy parental hands to the "old world" and instead touched carefully, so as not to damage the child's fragile psyche. It was not enough to deal with what the child did. We had to know what he felt, and why he felt it, and either way, we felt our own involvement. From bed-wetting to thumb-sucking to drug taking, new generations of parents believed it must have been something they did. While this fed heavily into parental guilt, it also suffocated many children's sense of self. Several single parents grew up with this kind of family style. Their dedication to their child's right to individual experiencing is often a direct result of their parents' oppressive overinvolvement with their own lives.

Ilse remembers endless "discussions" with her parents over her moods and feelings. "I used to pray that they'd just turn into the kinds of people who'd slap you if they thought you did something wrong, instead of these endless agonizing interpretations. Half the time I didn't know what they were talking about, but I'd accept their view of things. I think the thing I most resented," she said then, "was that I was never allowed to discover anything about myself on my own. I'd tell my mother something that I'd suddenly faced in myself, like that I didn't really hate swimming but I hated the way I looked in a bathing suit, and she'd give me that knowing smile, and say 'she'd known it all along.' She was always one step ahead of me. It made every personal discovery old hat and anti-climactic. . . ." Her voice trailed off, and when she spoke again, she was obviously experiencing some very old feelings of emotional distress. "I felt so cheated," she said. "I wanted to understand myself, not have someone else do it for me. I'd lie in my bed and hear my father and mother talking about me, sometimes arguing about me, and I wanted to scream. Why didn't they concentrate on their own lives instead of mine? God, how I hated my mother's preoccupation with everything I did. And it certainly hasn't made her happy. She blames herself for everything that went wrong with me and feels I'm not grateful enough to her for everything that went right. I'm never going to have that kind of relationship with my daughter," she said fiercely. "We have to relate to each other as independent people, not as a couple of psychological parasites."

The ability to break free of guilts associated with old ideas of parental responsibility affects how a single parent will manage her role. From Dr. Spock on down, most professional opinion, for or against the idea of single parenthood, will say that if the decision is made to be a single parent, it should at least be made positively and without guilt. One psychologist told of an unmarried patient who was so guilty about her decision that she found herself absolutely unable to discipline her child. She was so worried about "imposing" her style of parent on her daughter that she was unable to be a parent at all.

"The kid was a mess," the doctor said. "What she needed desperately was controls, a feeling that her mother was in charge and would help her through childhood. I believe a single parent is perfectly able to raise a psychologically healthy child. But they have to act like parents, and not be wistfully apologetic or overindulgent. Nothing makes a child more insecure than a parent who isn't sure of herself. I'd tell any single parent," he finished, "not to worry so much about what their kids are missing and concentrate instead on gaining self-confidence and assuming their own responsibilities."

Discipline and controls are, in fact, problems for some single parents. Despite their protests, there are sometimes feelings of guilt about the decision to raise their child with one instead of two parents. Or they may be rebelling against remembered rigidities of their own parents. And often, they are just simply too tired after a long day of work to put in the effort it can take to discipline well. Every parent knows that "giving in" is sometimes easier than holding out for what you know is more desirable behavior in the long run. Whatever the reason, some single parents will follow the "all right, *have* another cookie" style of parenting. The positive effects of delayed gratification are overlooked. This often has disastrous effects, some of them quite long-term.

It is important to remember that the origin of the word *discipline* means to *teach*—not to *punish*. A child, while having more inherent qualities than he has been credited for by some schools of psychology, still needs people to guide him toward a positive value system. One woman who runs a day-care center where two single mothers send their children, complained that her efforts to discipline their children in this positive way were constantly sabotaged by the mothers' overindulgence.

"They're both exactly the same," she said unhappily. "They can't say no to their children. They're so afraid of seeming like a witch in the few hours they have with their children at the end of a day. I can understand that," she said. "It's hard to leave a youngster all day and then come home and have to say no to things. But I really think the children are unconsciously testing them by their outrageous behavior to see how involved they actually are. It's my feeling that when a mother works, and especially a single mother, she has to be particularly firm and on top of things. Otherwise the child can really feel she's not engaged in his life at all. Even a child knows, and he knows it even while he's screaming and resisting the control, that his mother is much more involved when she says no to something that deserves a no, than when she lets him run wild."

Sometimes the problem area for a single mother is directly opposite to inadequate control. There is a tendency in single parent families, particularly when the parent is a single mother, to encourage excessive dependency in a child. Although women's liberation groups will argue that this behavior is not innate but conditioned by the culture, studies of a father's role in the family still picture him as a person who discourages any tendency in a mother to overprotect her child, and who directly encourages independence in the child himself.

Other studies have shown that there are two periods in a fatherless child's development when he is especially vulnerable to developing intense feelings of dependency on his mother. The first is at about nine months old, when he begins to test his mother to see if she will really meet his still great dependency needs. Does she come when he cries? Does she feed him when

THE PSYCHOLOGICAL EFFECTS OF HAVING A SINGLE PARENT 201

he's hungry? Erik Erikson considers the first year of life the time when a child begins to develop basic attitudes of either "trust" or "mistrust" toward the world, both in terms of other people, and in himself. This is, of course, one of the major reasons for a single parent to make provisions for really good child care if she has to work while her baby is still literally a baby. An infant whose needs are not met can begin to relate to the world with suspicion and fear, attitudes he may carry for a lifetime.

It is important to lovingly respond to a child of this age, but a single mother should also guard against being excessively hovering in her love. She wants her child to know he can depend on her, but she does not want him to begin feeling he cannot function without her.

Actually, the danger of overdependency occurs more in the second period mentioned, when the child is between two and three. Again, research into overdependency of children without fathers, corresponds with Erik Erikson's widely accepted views of the life stages all people experience. He sees this particular period of a child's life as a time when he will naturally begin to experiment with independence. Erikson refers to it as the period of "autonomy versus doubt." If a child is allowed to explore his own capabilities, to venture a little into the world beyond his mother's presence, he begins to feel capable of handling the world. If, instead, his mother rushes in to "protect" him, he may perceive the world as threatening and can begin to feel that without his mother's protection it would be a dangerous place to be. Therefore, investigative conclusions that many single mothers did tend to overprotect their children at this age, have special significance for mothers concerned that their children develop positive feelings of self.

Mothers on their own were found to be particularly overprotective in regard to possible physical injury to their children. Interestingly, several single mothers I talked to found themselves following this pattern, despite an intellectual awareness that it was "wrong." "I tried to analyze it," Jo Ann said, "and I think it has to do with the feeling I had of being so terribly *in* control all along. I mean I planned to have him and I'd managed everything by myself. Then all of a sudden he starts moving away from you, and so many other people and things are in his life, and you begin to realize just how out of control you really are. It's positively spooky. A hundred things could happen during a day that I have absolutely no influence on. I suppose it's sort of humbling, but it can also make you cling to the past and try to keep him under your thumb, where he's really been till now. . . ."

Marion faced this dilemma when she placed her daughter in family day care. The day-care mother lived in an apartment project that contained a large playground area.

"It was one of the reasons I chose this particular woman," Marion says ruefully, "and then it turned out to be the reason I almost ended the arrangement."

When her daughter reached the toddler stage, the day-care mother quite naturally took her downstairs to play every morning. One night Marion came to pick her up and saw a bruise on her forehead. The woman said another child had hit her with a toy, but that it had not broken the skin, and she had hardly cried.

"I felt a twinge, but I didn't say anything," Marion recalls. "But then, not long after, I came home and she had a cut on her wrist. She'd been playing on the swings and someone pushed her off. I really got very uptight. I remember that the next day it rained, and I was looking out my office window and suddenly felt relieved because I knew she wouldn't be outside playing!"

Her mid-week tensions carried over to the weekend, and when she took her daughter to the park near their own apartment, she would be on the alert for any "problems." She smilingly "encouraged" her daughter to play within her sight, and if she did wander away Marion was right behind her. At the first cry, she was up from the bench to see who had taken whose toy and to iron out the conflict before it intensified. She didn't stop to consider that it might have been resolved by the children themselves. After only a few weeks, both the day-care mother and Marion were conscious that the little girl was having much more difficulty playing than she'd had before. She would cry easily and leave the other children to come back to where mother or surrogate mother sat, quite obviously for reassurance that they were in fact still there.

The day-care mother broached the subject to Marion, "and it was all I needed to face the truth. I knew I'd been stifling any attempts she was making toward growing up, and I was making her afraid *to* grow up. At least I knew enough to stop—not to have her life limited by *my* fears."

To raise a child who has strong enough feelings of identity that he can move toward an unknown future with confidence is difficult but not impossible. And opinion has it that with enough ego strength of her own, a single parent can do as good a job as a married parent. In fact, many people feel that a single parent who tries to widen the circle of her child's sense of family, and who encourages the quality of independence, may be providing richer soil for the development of a strong identity than the nuclear family does.

Much is written today about identity confusion. It is, if we had to name one, probably the particular psychological problem of our time. Generally speaking, we can define identity as an integration of all the roles we've passed through and all we've learned from our developing experiences—to a point where we have an image of ourselves that is relatively clear. To be confused about our identity is to feel the opposite: to be unsure of who we are, where we belong, or who we want to relate to.

Our current cultural climate contributes to this identity confusion, and makes some particular problems for single parents and their children. We have broken continuity with past value systems and we are not sure what the new ones are. This is perhaps particularly apparent in terms of sexual identification for the single parent's child. Classic identity theory places great value on "appropriate" feelings of masculinity and femininity. Along with these feelings, of course, went related kinds of behavior. Girls were passive and boys were aggressive. Even recent writings on raising children in homes without mothers or fathers deal with how to develop "appropriate" gender behavior with the parent of that gender missing. At the same time new wave rhetoric assaults us with the idea that there is no such thing as appropriate gender behavior. We are, it says, if not one world, one people, and the fact that we have different sex organs implies nothing about our behavior. On this note, many psychiatrists feel that the current atmosphere of "you can't tell the boys from the girls" reflects young people's attempts to deal with their sexual confusion. One physician speculated in a professional paper that perhaps the unisex dress is a way of dealing with "the conflict in gender self-image . . . For in decreasing or eliminating the obvious differentiation between the sexes, the pressures to BE either male or female are lessened."

The question of the child's sexual identity has particular significance for the single parent. By *being* single parents, they are questioning many long-held assumptions about how we best develop sexual identity, such as by seeing "positive interactions" between a mother and father.

Yet as much in the vanguard of change as single parents are, they should be aware that as a society we are still very much in "process." The "product," which they may envision as a totally new sexual value system, has not yet arrived. Therefore the single parent, no matter how negatively she feels about sex-related definitions, should wait a while before abandoning every previously held opinion about the value of, or the best way to develop, strong feelings of sexual identity.

Research into the sexual attitudes of one-parent children concludes that "inappropriate" attitudes result less from having only one parent than from the attitudes of that parent. If single parents are in conflict about their feelings toward the opposite sex, their children may experience a variety of problems that relate to poor sexual identification. I say a variety of problems because a person's feeling about masculinity or femininity plays a significant role in the individual's overall feelings of a clear or confused identity. Many people in the psychological and sociological fields are concerned that in their attempts to be "equal," men and women who are single parents do not deny that there are differences between their male and female children.

This does not mean, of course, that we should go back to the old model of girls play with dolls and boys with trucks; although crusading single parents should not deny their children the opportunity to engage in particular activities, just because they do smack of earlier simplistic sex-role categorizing.

Alice, for example, the militant single mother, would have a hard time being the mother of a daughter. Her anger at a male-dominated society where girls were only "objects" would compel her to impose her egalitarian ideas of male-female behavior on a little girl—probably even more than she's doing now with her sons. As a matter of fact, her insistence that her sons never think of themselves as superior because they are males, plus her constant disparagement of every other male besides themselves promises some real problems. What will Alice do if one of the boys brings what Alice contemptuously calls a "toy girl" home someday?

"It won't be good," one psychiatrist said. "Women like Alice have a great investment in their children. They see them as their own symbol of change. But too often, I'm afraid, investments like these don't pay off. It's very conceivable that when the first girl comes along with shiny hair and eye makeup that the boy'll crumble. After all," he said with a smile, "sometimes it's nice to be looked up to instead of locked eyeball to eyeball in an even stare."

Rollo May has written that when individuals compulsively try to prove they are identical with a person of the opposite sex, they are open to a rather terrible "self-contradiction." Because in trying to be identical, you "repress your own unique sensibilities—and this is exactly what undermines your sense of identity."

For this reason, single parents such as Gary seem to be dealing with their children's sexual identities in particularly relevant and productive ways.

"I'm not concerned about male behavior, per se," Gary says. "What I'm really into is opening up the possibilities for how you can behave as a man." By way of explanation, he told of bursting into tears recently at the news that a good friend had died.

"My son walked into the room," Gary said, "and my instinct was to turn away. It's amazing how that 'Me Tarzan, You Jane' inculturation stays with you. I never saw my father shed a tear, even at my mother's funeral. And when I cried, he was very critical. I was a sissy, and I should be ashamed of myself. I *was,* by the way," Gary said with a smile. "And I'm going to show Mike that a boy, or a man, doesn't have to be ashamed if he shows emotions. That's really my point. It seems to me that feelings of inadequacy come from what people tell you you *can't* be as a male or female. As long as a boy can cry and still feel manly and a girl can assert herself and still be feminine, I don't think we have to deny that there are two sexes in the world and that in certain ways they're different from each other."

It is generally agreed that single parents should try to broaden, not obliterate, the definitions of male and female behavior both for themselves and for their children. A father who is comfortable about his manliness, and a mother who is comfortable about herself as a woman will be able to take on certain functions traditionally associated with the opposite sex. Doing this unself-consciously will then allow their children the widest range of behaviors within their own sex roles.

Sometimes it is not the opposite sex at large, but only one member that stands in the way of a single parent's relationship with the child. Again, this is often particularly true for a single mother of a natural son. Many single mothers insist that the child's father is irrelevant to their feelings about being a mother. But the question should be considered of whether we can really see a child totally separate from the man who helped create him. If a boy too much resembles his natural father, and if that resemblance is associated with emotional pain, the mother may consciously or unconsciously reject her child. Her son's developing masculinity will awaken old resentments, and can quite negatively influence the mother-child relationship.

The issues of overprotection and sexuality are connected again when we look at the intensity of the single mother's relationship with her child, once more particularly with her sons. Earlier studies into single parent families found that overprotective mothers tended to have a great deal of physical contact with their sons. A number of single mothers, for example, shared their bedrooms with their children. This is a sleeping arrangement to be abandoned as early in a boy's life as possible. While theories about homosexuality are changing, as are interpretations of its "pathology," studies do show that a very close maternal relationship, with much physical contact, does interfere with heterosexual adjustments. Single mothers are strongly advised not to confuse maternal warmth and affection with expressions of love that are tinged with seductiveness or are excessively intense. The same would, of course, hold true for single fathers and daughters. There is actually comparatively little research about single parents of either sex in relation to daughters. But what there is clearly indicates that for both boys and girls, overprotection or rejection of sex-related expressions of self, will interfere with the child's healthy psychological development.

Much of this research and its conclusions relates to the classic psychologic theory of the Oedipal complex. Most behaviorists maintain a belief in these theories, even though they update them in terms of newer perceptions of personality. Briefly, the Oedipal complex involves the idea that a mother is a child's first love object and source of identification. Between the ages of three to six, a child idealizes his parents. They are ten feet tall, beautiful, all powerful, and all knowing. A boy of this age patterns himself after his father. His mother is the quintessent woman. He romanticizes her glories way out of proportion with reality. A four-year-old boy wants to be just like his father and marry his mother. At the same time, however, the boy resents his father because of his prior claim on that magnificent female. So a child of this age is a jumble of feelings. They involve almost equal amounts of love and hostility —plus guilt over the hostility and fear that he will be punished for daring to feel it.

The Oedipus conflict in a boy begins to be resolved when he accepts the fact that he really cannot trade places with his father. Instead he concentrates more on identifying with him and replicating many of his behaviors. At the same time, he becomes more independent of his mother and starts moving toward adulthood where he can form romantic attachments with other more appropriate love figures. Concern for the single mother with a son is that this period of development will not be "worked through." The boy may, as suggested, remain too close to his mother with resulting confusion about his own role. A number of professional people attribute homosexuality in both men and women to unresolved Oedipal conflicts.

Ruth, the single mother who had no relationships with any men during her son's growing up, illustrates the dangers of making the mother-son relationship too binding for too long a time. Ruth's son was showing clear signs of sexual confusion. He was overly attached to his mother and had affected many mannerisms his classmates jeeringly labeled as "queer." At the urging of friends, Ruth took him for professional help, largely because the boy was obviously unhappy. Their first visit with the therapist was quite rocky, with the boy showing immediate dislike for the man. In her naïveté, Ruth assured the doctor that her son reacted this way with all men and "not to take it personally."

The doctor recognized the boy's antagonism toward any man who took some of his mother's attention away. He urged that Ruth enter therapy herself, where eventually she realized that she was actually discouraging her son from masculine development. Her own ambivalence about sex and men caused her to do this. Without realizing what she was doing, or why, she continuously reinforced her son's dependency. He was approved of and rewarded for being docile, passive, and obedient—and punished for being assertive or what his mother called "willful."

The results of Ruth's life of isolation with her son point up the necessity for providing role models of the opposite sex for a child to identify with. This, again, is true for both sons and daughters of single parents. In the area of complexes there is equality among the sexes.

The little girl sees her father as the love object, and her mother the person blocking her attempts to get him. Called the Electra complex, this stage of emotional development brings the same kinds of conflicts to the child. If a father is absent then, a girl will also have no opportunity to form an initial sexual attachment, or work its complex feelings through. So significant relationships with people of the opposite sex from the parent are important for a single parent's child. And it should be a person who is around consistently so that the child can act out some of his feelings and begin to resolve them.

A father with a girl can also provide a kind of affirmation of her femaleness that many psychiatrists feel is crucial to her own sexuality. Frigidity is often seen as a component of poor or missing father-daughter relationships. While seductiveness is unhealthy between a parent and child, an air of "sensuousness," according to one psychiatrist I talked to, allows a girl to discover her femininity. No matter how far we move in equality of the sexes, a man will probably treat a little girl quite specially—and it is a special treatment that may be at least partially significant to her later feelings about herself as a woman. No matter how well a woman feels able to live without a man in her life, she should not rob her children of the important opportunity to relate to men in their own lives.

This is really the thread that runs through the entire discussion of the psychological adjustment of a single parent's child. The parent has separated herself from marriage, but she has also separated her child from some of society's experiences. The child will need continuing assistance in adjusting to his own uniqueness. For example, what do you tell a child about his life-style? Most single parents find that direct statements are the best arguments. It is important that the child understand that his parent's decision not to marry had nothing to do with love for him. If the father is present in his life, questions about his parents' situation should be answered honestly in terms of the adults' feelings about each other. And they should be careful that he not get the idea that he was the cause of their deciding not to legally commit themselves to the relationship. If the father is not on the scene, a mother can simply tell her child that for whatever reason is closest to the truth, marriage was not feasible for her. Many people feel that a child's sense of loss about a missing parent can be well compensated for by his mother's obvious commitment to being his parent. And it is "obvious," most single parents feel, because it was a role they so deliberately chose.

"How can he not understand how committed I am to him?" Jo-Ann asked. "As soon as he's old enough to realize the alternatives—that I could have had an abortion or given him up for adoption—he has to understand that I chose the most difficult alternative. That I did, and that we're happy with each other, should be clear enough evidence of how deeply I love him."

Strangely, some professionals feel that the adopted child may have a particular difficulty in resolving the conflict about being a single parent's child. The classic answer to a child's questions of why his natural mother gave him up for adoption was that his mother was not married. But as the adopted child of a single parent, that answer no longer works. When Betty's daughter first broached the question, Betty found herself answering with the usual cause-and-effect response. "But then, of course, I realized what a specious argument that was from me —even at her age, she asked me, 'But you're not married either. Why didn't my other mommy keep me like you are?' "

Betty then amended her answer to a specific discussion of some of the reasons the "other mommy" could not raise her as well as Betty. Not enough money, health, and the like.

"They were instinctive responses, but I'm going to have to figure out a much more real and valid set of answers for her when she's older. Otherwise I think she may feel a sense of real deprivation and abandonment."

A recent study of the children of unwed mothers indicated that in comparison to another group of study children who had

THE PSYCHOLOGICAL EFFECTS OF HAVING A SINGLE PARENT

fathers, they did not show significantly greater symptoms of emotional problems. Out of forty-two symptoms covered by the study, only four showed a really significant difference between the two groups of children. It is interesting, though, to note that the major difference, attributed to twice as many children of single mothers as married mothers, was fear of separation.

The single mother has, of course, separated herself from many of society's values. And in a way, she and the single father may see their children as the children of tomorrow. But they should keep in mind that for today, at least, these children are still children. They may not be ready yet for their parents' emancipation from society and social or psychological history. Single parents are forging new answers, but their children are asking a very old question, Who am I? As children of a transitional age, and standing dead center in the spotlight of change, they need thoughtful help from their parents to be confident about developing their own answers.

Creating Tomorrow's Person

THERE IS A GREAT TEMPTATION in times of change to try and relate the present to the past. To try and find in our current chaos something familiar. To then be able to say, "Of course, people have always been rebellious, or unconventional; other periods have been, in their way, just as confusing." This rationalization allows us to rest a while, to sit patiently in the wings until those crazy people in the middle of things come to their senses.

Nevertheless, the three-cornered hat of our traditional code, God, the Flag, and Motherhood, has been squashed out of any possible resemblance to its old stiff shape. This is not to suggest that we are heading toward total amorality. Many of us will continue to believe in one or all of these values, although our belief is newly individual and continuously open to modification.

I suggest simply that the changes in society today are unique, both because of the speed at which they take place and the widespread range of their effects. The obsolescence level of every aspect of our life gets shorter every day. From commodities to moralities, the life-span shrinks, and the discard pile grows higher.

It is important to accept the uniqueness of our age in order to understand the phenomenon of the single parent. Her behavior must be seen against a background that today careens wildly in all directions. If we place her in front of yesterday's steadier landscape, then we can easily dismiss her as being some cultural aberration, interesting, but not terribly important to the culture as a whole.

But a person's behavior, and even her problems, can only be viewed in relation to her total environment. There is a growing awareness of this fact in professional circles, and modern psychiatry often incorporates many tenets of other disciplines, such as sociology and even economics. As one psychiatrist said, "You can't any longer place therapist and patient in a 'locked twosome' in the sanctified atmosphere of the treatment room." The outside world's problems are too pervasive and the individual tensions that brought patient to therapy inevitably reflect the tensions of the entire society. In the same way, in a world of shifting values we cannot easily dismiss any value system as being so obviously deviant that it is irrelevant to our own lives.

Some time ago, Margaret Mead was interviewed on that favorite topic of the generation gap. By way of illustration she talked of a scientist friend of hers who was having a particularly frustrating discussion with his young son. Suddenly, however, the father understood what their communication problem was. He realized, Dr. Mead reported, that as an adult, he was "standing on the earth, looking at the moon," while his son, born into a decade of unparalleled technology, was "standing on the moon, looking at the earth." So the single parent, as other people experimenting with 1973's freedoms, must be evaluated from the moon's side. This is often hard. To someone inculturated before World War II, it is almost impossible to understand why a person would want to be a parent without marriage. This, by the way, makes the older single parents particularly courageous members of the brave new world. They are going so very far away from the value system of most of their peers. Both Betty and Jean have friends who dropped them abruptly after their decisions to adopt a child. And in Betty's case, a few more suddenly disappeared when the child turned out to be interracial.

Younger people, even if they themselves choose more conventional life-styles, can usually relate to their contemporaries who have passed tradition by. "I just like the idea of marriage," one young bride told me. "I suppose to many people my age, I'm very square and ridiculously old-fashioned. . . ." Her voice trailed off, sounding kind of sheepish. But then she went on to tell me that she was, first of all, not as young as she seemed. She turned twenty-five on her wedding day, and had been living alone for three years before this. And finally, she had lost her virginity at the age of seventeen. If she is a "square" in the current idiom, it is a new idiom indeed. And here we can see how the single parent is both caused by and affects the culture she is part of. Her experiments with freedom are only experiments further along the scale of experimentation that everyone is, if not involved in, at least touched by. The girl who married at twenty-five, for example, reflects the growing number of girls who are delaying marriage until their mid-twenties. This was an age when, until a short time ago, she would already have had a couple of legally blessed children.

A correlation is made between the higher age of marriage and the frequent decision not to have too many or even any children —a decision that was unthinkable not too long ago. A sociologist makes the point that if a girl marries in her mid-twenties she may conceivably be established in a career, and would have already experienced herself in a variety of ways as a person. "She may not need that definition of self being pregnant often means to a young inexperienced bride," he said.

The divorce rate escalates daily and the reasons for divorce multiply. Again, reflecting how language makes its own adjustment to change, the word *divorce* is becoming obsolete, unable to really suggest its contemporary implications. For this reason, under a Family Law Act in California, as of January 1, 1970, divorce courts have outlawed *divorce* and substituted the word *dissolution.* Supporters of the law feel this semantic change makes the language more relevant to what the end of a marriage really means today. In California there is no longer a guilty party and an abused party, pointing fingers at each other as they list their grievances. Those catchall catechisms of love gone sour—adultery, mental cruelty, desertion—have been abandoned. In their place, a couple simply decide they no longer want to live together as man and wife. The language of their brief for dissolution reads only that there are "irreconcilable differences."

The point of all this is that a general movement exists toward reexamining priorities and value systems. The single parent is then only a specific symbol of that movement. Understanding this, understanding how cultural influences have helped create the single parent, we can try to make some assessment of how the single parent will herself affect the culture.

As already noted, the single parent comes in a variety of styles. Few that I personally talked to had particularly messianic views of their decisions. They were far more involved with making each day count in highly personal ways than they were in forging complicated plans for society tomorrow. Some psychiatrists, however, believe that many people who put themselves in the vanguard of change are at least unconsciously trying to lead their culture down particular paths. Whether or not this is so, a larger question remains, Does the single parent have any influence, and what kind, on the world she and her child are part of?

Consensus is that single parents and their children will both have real influences on the general culture. In the parent's breaking of tradition, and in the child's growing up without these traditions, society is shown that alternate behaviors are both possible and plausible. When tradition is challenged even by a few, change becomes conceivable for many, because the inviolate qualities of tradition have lessened. As soon as a moral code or ethic is debated, it loses some of its power. The awe-inspiring qualities of sanctified robes are lost in the street clothes of open debate. The moment we can question a "truth," it becomes less absolutely "true" and we no longer feel impelled to live by its code.

This, then, is the most important way that the single parent is likely to affect her society. She has broken tradition, and by doing so has changed the value of tradition. It is conceivable that some children of single parents will as a possible route of rebellion, or by personal preference, become conservative and believers in the status quo. The vast majority, however, will probably be people who are at least comparatively loose-jointed and flexible. They may not be less neurotic than children of more traditional homes, but their particular problems will generally not stem from white-knuckled attempts to grasp on to certainties.

And here is another important concept of how single parents affect society. Their behavior puts new focus on the idea of change as a positive value. A family, and a culture, socializes its members to adjust to and maintain its existing social structures. But how do you socialize people into a world where the structures are shifting? These are different times from those in which our lives were measured by generationally familiar way stations. We are almost totally separating ourselves from the idea that tomorrow is only an extension of yesterday, or even of today. It used to be that parents would aim their children toward a life that was perhaps more ambitious than their own, but was in its most important ways recognizable. Country doctors wanted their sons to be big city specialists. Mothers who lived in five-room apartments hoped their daughters would marry well and move to ten-room houses. But in the same way that a parent of twenty-five years ago could not prepare a child for single parenthood, parents today, single or married, cannot draw a meaningful map for any part of their children's trips into the future. We cannot conceptualize the unknown. For this reason, on a parent-to-child level and on a culture-to-members level, many authorities now feel that the only valid socialization is to show people how to be flexible enough to enter the unknown unafraid.

Many sociologists believe that some of the more violent revolutionary behavior today results from young people not having learned that change can come about in nonviolent ways. Never having had, according to a report delivered by Elise Boulding at the 1971 annual meeting of the American Orthopsychiatric Association, "success experiences with activist behavior," and lacking "other supportive experiences or role models, they may come to feel that destruction is a necessary precondition of change." The report, titled "Socialization Sequences and Student Attitudes Towards Non-Violent Social Change," went on to speculate that if, on the other hand, a culture placed a higher value on change, "a larger percentage of young people growing up in that society will respond to possible change roles. . . ."

As opinion grows that the way to exist in a transitional age is to be adaptable to the new, rather than to aggrandize the old, the single parent can be seen as a significant change agent for the culture she or he is part of. Their children will grow up in an atmosphere that itself is a metaphor for this view of life. Even theologians say today that morality has a newly relativistic quality. If we agree to this, then the single parent, who was able to determine a personal morality and live by it, may be an important moral role model for her child. This, despite the fact that her way of life is by today's conventional standards, "immoral."

"I would no more tell a person that a particular way of life was "bad" than I would say I knew the one way that was "good," a minister told me. "Obviously," he went on, "a single parent who was a caring and responsible parent cannot be considered immoral in comparison with the married woman who is neglectful of her children. It's absurd to think we can give a child a set of fixed rules to live by in a world that has so many alternate standards."

This man, as many of his religious peers, felt that the parental obligation in the area of morality was to help a child develop enough self-respect and confidence to determine his own rules in a way that is not destructive to other members of society. By its very definition, this attitude suggests again enormous flexibility and fluid, relative judgments. What would be wrong at one time in one place, would be right in another. How to distinguish what time, what place, under what circumstances, places great responsibility on each individual. Whole generations of lives have been built on codes that said, "This is what I ought to do." Less and less do we believe in "oughts" on any universal basis. Now, and in the future, we have to say, each in his own voice, "This is what I choose to do."

The idea of fluidity, of separate rather than fixed judgments, implies that certain kinds of people will be better prepared to live in a world where directions are uncertain than others. Psychologists recall the old belief that we reached a particular kind of identity early in life, and lived that way till we died. We were this or that kind of person, and people could count on us to respond in particular ways. Like Grant Wood figures, we remained in just about one emotional position for a lifetime.

Now, on the other hand, authorities tell us that several identities can be experienced during a life. In fact, they *must* be assumed, or we will not be able to cope with changing realities. In politics, business, sex, education, so much "accepted" belief suddenly becomes obsolete. Unless we are able to move on to the new, live with it a while, and then move on again, we too are likely to become obsolete, petulantly telling "how it used to be" to an empty room.

If enough people find themselves unable to cope with the stresses of their culture, the culture itself is threatened. If society is to remain viable then, it must develop people who can respond to its needs, and who can handle the particular tools those needs involve. The tools for living today include the ability to question rather than accept, to be adaptable, to experiment, to be ready to abandon old answers willingly, and to be always open to new ones. Recent studies into the people who become campus activists in positive nonviolent ways arrived at some interesting related conclusions. They found this group of people to be, in comparison to their more quiescent peers, "flexible, tolerant, and realistic . . . less dependent on authority rules or rituals for managing social relationships." They were also, according to the report, people who have a personal value system that combines a concern for self-expression with a feeling of community for others. Nonactivists, on the other hand, were found to be people interested in personal success, and were what in more passive days might have been assessed more positively as "self-denying, conventional, competitive, self-controlled, foresighted, and orderly."

According to the old definition, the single parent certainly is not being "orderly." She has reversed priorities and is not lining everything up neatly at all. Some single parents, of course, do replicate the most traditional home. Meals are served on time, laundry is stacked neatly in drawers, bedtime is fixed. But the majority of people who have reached parenthood from a new combination of ideas have personal ideas of how important any set of rules and regulations are in life. It is this very disregard of some of child-raising's sacred codes that some psychiatrists feel is particularly valuable to the single parent's child.

"A parent who isn't 'perfect,'" one psychiatrist said, "makes it easier for a child. Those paragons so many nuclear parents felt they had to be, always above suspicion, always the keeper of the 'truth,' were an incredible burden for most kids. A mother would grit her teeth and do all kinds of things around a house and for her child that she hated in order to live up to her mythical idea of the good mother. Meanwhile the kid was living with a plaster statue who never came down to any human level in any consistent way. How could a child not expect to fall short of such perfection himself? Or ever really get past the perfection for real intimacy?"

The doctor then explained that having a parent who had broken society's traditions, and who was experimenting with life, could remove some of the "pomposity" from the parental role. Experimentation, he said, always carries at least the possibility of failure, and this possibility brings the parent down to more human scale.

The key to this positive view of single parenthood, however, is the feeling that the parent must truly be committed to her child. Critics of the single parent experience are concerned over the fact that the child is not seeing his parent make a firm commitment to another adult.

"Certainly many, perhaps most, marriages are not truly happy," a marriage counselor said to me. "But if the people aren't severely neurotic, they are at least trying to make something work within its institutions. A child who is raised in an environment where he sees his parents often sublimating personal needs for the greater goal of keeping the marriage and family together, *I* think is getting an important model for his own life. A parent who can whimsically abandon a partner seems to be saying that she's not willing to make much of an investment in anything that doesn't solve immediate gratification needs. Unless," he concluded, "she really is committed to the child's welfare in some way more than to her own, I think she will be leaving a great blind spot in the child's view of life and relationships."

Several other people in the psychological field were concerned about this aspect of continuing commitment to another person, as an aspect the single parent's child might not see. "I don't mean to sound like yesterday's puritan," a psychiatrist said, "but I am concerned that we don't lose entirely the idea that life isn't all taking and no giving. Anyone who's involved with people's emotional life as I am knows that there's a growing feeling of alienation, from self as well as others. I think much of it has to do with giving up the idea that we have to pay a certain price for satisfactions, that in fact, the satisfaction is often increased if you do pay a price. This hit-and-run grabbing-off-the-counter attitude so many young people seem to have suggests they have no real opportunity to feel connected with any goals. I would think," he continued, "that a single parent would have to really substitute a solid framework of values and commitments to make up for what isn't there in the form of a marriage."

Any discussion of where single parents and their children fit into society seems to come full circle to the fact that, first of all, they *are* single. They are people who, for various reasons, have not married. Are they then, a mirror in which we can see reflected major changes in the future shape of marriage? Will we perhaps one day not see any reflection at all? Can marriage survive in a culture that is in such turbulent transition?

Most experts in the field, whether they wear the badges of conservative or revolutionary, feel marriage will survive as an institution, but that it will in fact, bear little resemblance to the institution it used to be. Not only will there be all kinds of variations on the traditional model, the model itself will lose much of its status-related significance. For marriage will cease to be so hallowed or exclusive a club. Membership will be clearly optional, and the "ins" will be just as respected as the "outs." The days when we felt sorry for people who went through life single are clearly over. Too many routes to personal fulfillment are open for us to believe that only the old route of marriage is the "right way."

The child of single parents will, of course, know there are alternatives to marriage. But the child of most marriages will learn this too. For if the single parent has separated parenthood from marriage, the culture as a whole is separating love from marriage. The *New York Times* in May, 1972, featured a story on how many middle-class parents are, with varying degrees of discomfort, allowing their teen-age children to openly conduct sexual relationships. Sons and daughters home from college with a friend of the opposite sex take for granted they will pass up the prim propriety of the guest room and share instead their own familiar bedroom. And while few of these young people are promiscuous, chances are that the same expectation will hold for several other "friends" before the college years are over.

When the culture precluded positive sexual relationships with people we did not have deep commitments to, we had to convince ourselves that every potential bedmate was worthy of the experience. And by worthy we did not mean just liking them or being attracted to them, or even loving them. At least loving them in the free-flowing connotations the word has today. Love came wrapped in wedding rings and mortgages, and anything less was only imitation. Therefore, if we could not satisfy sexual needs honorably by being in love, we had to convince ourselves we were in love. And if love meant marriage, then we married. "Better wed than dead-ened" by frustration or guilt.

Now, men and women are beginning to make relationships that are freed from false illusion and self-deception. They can love each other, if they are self-sufficient people, without contractual promises that they will always be "loved" in return. Confidence in yourself as a total person allows you to meet other people in an atmosphere of mutual freedom. Some of these relationships will end in marriage. Others will not. In marriage and out, the relationships will last for varying periods of time.

The pattern of the single parent's life is new; particularly new in that it is cut to individual order. Whether the choice is to marry or not marry, to have children or not, to go to college or not—the word that is the true password to tomorrow is *choice*. Knocking on the glass door, behind which we can see such unlimited landscapes, we want to say not that anyone "sent us," but that we came here all by ourselves. Everywhere people are demanding the right to choose. They insist on alternatives, demand options.

Into this world the child of the single parent grows. Will he be better equipped to move with its rhythms than the child of more traditional families? Living with innovation, will he be particularly free to himself be an innovator? No one really can be certain yet. Most children of single parents are still very young. Whether the particular stresses of being a kind of marginal person, straddling the value systems of two eras, will limit his chances for positive experience, again is still only speculation. Most single parents, though, are not worried about this aspect of their decisions.

"Good Lord," Rebecca said. "It's not as if I'm raising her to marry the boy next door!" And then she broke out laughing. "Well," she said, giggling, "maybe I am. But the boy next door in this case has a black father who's a dancer and a white mother who's a sculptor. I really don't think it's going to hassle them very much that I never married."

On this note, it seems worthwhile to say one final time that we cannot look at the single parent with anything but today's wider angle of vision. An acquaintance once came home from a first trip to Italy and said that it was very nice, but "everyone spoke Italian." If we continue to think that there should be a universal tongue, our own, and that any other behavioral language is "foreign," and therefore "deviant," we can never make any fair assessment of the single parent experience.

In our lack of objectivity, we may be hurting ourselves most of all. Like it or not, the sea of change catches us all in its wake, diver and toe dipper alike. In such uncharted waters, we are foolish to be elitest about who we are willing to swim with. Especially when some of those people are far bolder swimmers than we are yet ready to be. We can move slowly and learn from their mistakes. But we should also realize that in many ways we are profiting from their strengths.

Appendix

State Sources for Adoption, Pregnancy, and Related Legal Counseling

ALABAMA

Commissioner
State Department of Pensions and Security
Attention: Bureau of Child Welfare
Administrative Building
64 North Union Street
Montgomery, Alabama 36104

ALASKA

Director
Department of Health and Welfare
Division of Public Welfare
Pouch H
Juneau, Alaska 99801

ARIZONA

Director
Department of Public Welfare
State Office Building
Phoenix, Arizona 85007

ARKANSAS

Director
Arkansas State Department
  of Public Welfare
Box 1437
Little Rock, Arkansas 72203

CALIFORNIA

Commissioner
State Department of Social Welfare—Social
  Service Division
744 P Street
Sacramento, California 95814

COLORADO

State Department of Social Services
Attention: Director of Family
  and Children Section
1575 Sherman Street
Denver, Colorado 80203

CONNECTICUT

Commissioner of Social Services
State Welfare Department
1000 Asylum Avenue
Hartford, Connecticut 06105

DELAWARE

Director
Division of Social Services
Box 309
Wilmington, Delaware 19899

DISTRICT OF COLUMBIA

Director
Social Services Administration
122 C Street N.W.
Washington, D.C. 20001

FLORIDA

Director
Division of Family Services
P O Box 2050
Jacksonville, Florida 32203

GEORGIA

Director
Division for Children and Youth
State Office Building
Capitol Square
Atlanta, Georgia 30334

HAWAII

Director
Family Services
Department of Social Services
P O Box 339
Honolulu, Hawaii 96809

IDAHO

Director
Bureau of Family and Children's Services
State Department of Public Assistance
Box 1189
Boise, Idaho 83701

ILLINOIS

Director
Division of Child Welfare
Illinois Department of Children
  and Family Services
528 South Fifth Street
Springfield, Illinois 62706

APPENDIX 229

INDIANA

Director
Children's Division
State Department of Public Welfare
100 North Senate Avenue
Indianapolis, Indiana 46204

IOWA

Director
Bureau of Family and Children's Services
Iowa Department of Social Services
Lucas State Office Building
Des Moines, Iowa 50319

KANSAS

Director
Child Welfare Services
State Department of Social Welfare
State Office Building
Topeka, Kansas 66612

KENTUCKY

Director
Department of Child Welfare
403 Wapping Street
Frankfort, Kentucky 40601

LOUISANA

Commissioner
Child Welfare
Department of Public Welfare
P O Box 44065
Baton Rouge, Louisiana 70804

MAINE

Director
Bureau of Social Welfare
State Department of Health and Welfare
State House
August, Maine 04330

MARYLAND

Director
Family and Child Welfare Services
Social Services Administration—Department
  of Employment and Social Services
1100 North Eutow Street
Baltimore, Maryland 21201

MASSACHUSETTS

Director
Social Services
Massachusetts Department of Public Welfare
600 Washington Street
Boston, Massachusetts 02111

APPENDIX

MICHIGAN

Director
State Department of Social Services
300 South Capitol
Lansing, Michigan 48926

MINNESOTA

Director
Division of Child Welfare
Minnesota Department of Public Welfare
Centennial Office Building
Saint Paul, Minnesota 55101

MISSISSIPPI

Director
Division of Family and Children's Services
State Department of Public Welfare
Box 4321
Fondren Station
Jackson, Mississippi 39216

MONTANA

Director
Division of Social Services
State Department of Public Welfare
Helena, Montana 59601

NEBRASKA

Director
Division of Social Services
Department of Public Welfare
1526 K Street
Lincoln, Nebraska 68508

NEVADA

Director
State Department of Health, Welfare,
 and Rehabilitation
515 East Musser Street
Carson City, Nevada 89701

NEW HAMPSHIRE

Director
State Department of Health and Welfare
Division of Welfare
1 Pillsbury Street
Concord, New Hampshire 03301

NEW JERSEY

Director
Bureau of Children's Services
Division of Public Welfare
State Department of Institutions
 and Agencies
P O Box 510
Trenton, New Jersey 08625

NEW MEXICO

Chief
Family and Children's Services Section
Social and Rehabilitation Services Division
Health and Social Services Department
P O Box 2348
Santa Fe, New Mexico 87501

NEW YORK

Commissioner
New York State Department of Social Services
1450 Western Avenue
Albany, New York 12203

NORTH CAROLINA

Commissioner
State Department of Social Services
P O Box 2599
Raleigh, North Carolina 27602

NORTH DAKOTA

Director
Social Services
Department of Social Service
Capitol Building
Bismarck, North Dakota 58501

OHIO

Chief
Bureau of Family and Children's Services
State Department of Public Welfare
408 East Town Street
Columbus, Ohio 43215

OKLAHOMA

Director
State Department of Institutions
Social and Rehabilitative Services
P O Box 25352
Oklahoma City, Oklahoma 73125

OREGON

Director
Services to Families and Adult Section
State Department
Public Welfare Division
422 Public Service Building
Salem, Oregon 97310

PENNSYLVANIA

Director
Bureau of Family and Child Welfare
Office of Family Services
State Department of Public Welfare
Harrisburg, Pennsylvania 17120

APPENDIX

PUERTO RICO

Director
Services to Families and Children
Family Services
Department of Social Services
P O Box 11697
Fernandez Juncos Station
Santurce, Puerto Rico 00910

RHODE ISLAND

Director
Rhode Island Child Welfare Service
610 Mount Pleasant Avenue
Providence, Rhode Island 02908

SOUTH CAROLINA

Chief
Division of Children and Family Services
State Department of Public Welfare
Box 1520
Columbia, South Carolina 29202

SOUTH DAKOTA

Director
Service Administration
State Department of Public Welfare
Pierre, South Dakota 57501

TENNESSEE

Director
Social Services
State Department of Public Welfare
410 State Office Building
Nashville, Tennessee 37219

TEXAS

Commissioner
State Department of Public Welfare
John H. Reagan Building
Austin, Texas 78701

UTAH

Chief
Bureau of Family and Children's Services
Division of Family Services
231 East Fourth Street
Salt Lake City, Utah 84111

VERMONT

Director
Children's Services Division
State Department of Social Welfare
Montpelier, Vermont 05602

VIRGINIA

Chief
Bureau of Family and Children's Services
State Department of Welfare and Institutions
429 South Belvidere Street
Richmond, Virginia 23220

WASHINGTON

Director
Division of Public Assistance
Department of Social and
 Health Services
P O Box 1788
Olympia, Washington 98501

WEST VIRGINIA

Director
Division of Social Services
State Department of Welfare
State Office Building
1900 Washington Street
East Charleston, West Virginia 25305

WISCONSIN

Administrator
Division of Family Services
Department of Health and Social Services
State Office Building
Madison, Wisconsin 53702

WYOMING

Director
Family and Children's Services
Division of Public Assistance
  and Social Services
State Office Building
Cheyenne, Wyoming 82001

These agencies will refer people to local county and city bureaus.

INFORMATION DIRECTORIES

For the person who is considering becoming a single parent, libraries will generally carry directories that supply information about community resources, such as:

The Annual Directory of United Way of America
This publication lists the community service councils and voluntary agencies within the state.

The National Directory of Private Social Agencies

The Annual Directory of the Child Welfare League's Member Agencies

Bibliography

Alger, Ian, M.D., "Marriage—The Great Substitute." Forum Lecture, Cooper Union, October 16, 1968.

Dempsey, David, "The Mead and Her Message." *New York Times Magazine,* 1970.

The Double Jeopardy—The Triple Crisis-Illegitimacy Today. Booklet, New York: National Council on Illegitimacy, 1969.

Edmiston, Susan, "The Psychology of Day Care." *New York Magazine,* Vol. 4, No. 14, April 5, 1971.

Egleson, Jim and Frank, Janet, *Parents Without Partners,* New York: E.P. Dutton, 1961.

Ferguson, Elizabeth, Ph.D., "The Social Revolution in Sexual Behavior and Standards." *Illegitimacy,* publication of National Council on Illegitimacy, New York, October, 1965.

Feurey, Joe and Taubman, Bryna, "Singles in New York." *New York Post,* October 22, 1969.

Halleck, Seymour, M.D., "The Uses of 'Abnormality'—A Psychiatric Reappraisal." *Current Magazine,* published in Vermont by Goddard Publications, July-August, 1971.

Haselkorn, Florence, Editor, *Family Planning—Readings and Case Materials*. New York: Council on Social Work Education, 1971.

"Interview with a Homosexual Spokesman." *Sexual Behavior,* New York: Interpersonal Publications, Vol. 1, No. 8, November, 1971.

Jones, Ernest, *The Life and Work of Sigmund Freud*. New York: Basic Books, 1961.

Jones, Eve, *Raising Your Child in a Fatherless Home*. New York: Macmillan Company, 1963.

Kadushin, Alfred, "Single-Parent Adoptions: An Overview and Some Relevant Research." *Social Service Review,* Vol. 44, No. 3, Chicago: The University of Chicago Press, September, 1970.

Kantor, Rosabeth, "Getting It All Together; Some Group Issues in Communes."Paper delivered to the American Orthopsychiatric Association, Washington, D.C., 1971.

Klein, Jenny W., "Educational Component of Day Care." *Children Today,* DHEW Publication, Vol. 1, No. 1, January-February, 1972.

Klein, Ted, *The Fathers' Book*. New York: Ace Publishing Company, 1968.

Klemer, Richard H., *Marriage and Family Relationships*. New York: Harper and Row, 1970.

Knight, James A., M.D., "Unusual Case: False Pregnancy In A Male." *Medical Aspects of Human Sexuality,* Vol. V, No. 3, March, 1971.

Levine, Saul V., M.D., "The Urban Commune: Fact or Fad, Promise or Pipe Dream." Research Paper, presented to the American Orthopsychiatric Association Annual Meeting, Detroit, April, 1972.

Linner, Birgitta, "What Does Equality Between the Sexes Imply?" Research paper, American Orthopsychiatric Association, March 22, 1971.

Mead, Margaret, *Culture and Committment*. New York: Natural History Press, Doubleday, 1970.

Morgenstern, Joseph, "The New Face of Adoption." *Newsweek Magazine,* September 13, 1971.

Ostrovsky, Everett S., *Children Without Men.* New York: G.P. Putnam, 1959.

Reische, Diana, Editor, *Women and Society.* New York: H.W. Wilson Company, 1972.

Roberts, Steven V., "Supply of Adoptable White Babies Shrinks." *New York Times,* July 18, 1971.

Rosenhan, David, "Some Origins of Concern for Others." Research Paper, Center for Psychological Studies, The Educational Testing Service, Princeton, N.J.

Rubin, Isadore, "Transition in Sex Values—Implications for the Education of Adolescents." Journal of Marriage and the Family, Vol. 27, No. 2, May, 1965.

Sauber, Mignon and Corrigan, Eileen M., "The Six-Year Experience of Unwed Mothers as Parents." Study published by the Community Council of Greater New York, Research Department, 1970.

"Single Motherhood." *Time Magazine,* September 6, 1971.

Skolnick, Arlene S., Jerome H., *Family in Transition.* Boston: Little, Brown and Company, 1971.

Spock, Benjamin, M.S., *Dr. Spock Talks About Problems of Parents.* New York: Crest Books, 1962.

Unmarried Parents and Their Children, Trends, Challenges, Concerns. Collected and made available by the Child Welfare League. New York: Symposium in honor of Florence Kreech, Executive Director of Louise Wise Services. Speakers: Joseph H. Reid, Walter A. Heath, Samuel C. Bullock, M.D., Viola W. Bernard, M.D., October, 1969.

Young, Leontine, *Out of Wedlock.* New York: McGraw Hill, 1954.

Wilson, Theo, "The Adoption Underground." Series of articles, *New York Daily News,* July, 1971.